CARING
FOR THE
EARTH

A STRATEGY FOR SURVIVAL

CARING
FOR THE
EARTH

A STRATEGY FOR SURVIVAL

Published in association with:
IUCN – The World Conservation Union
UNEP – United Nations Environment Programme
WWF – World Wide Fund For Nature

Mitchell Beazley

IUCN
The World Conservation Union

UNEP

WWF

General editor and writer
Roger Few

Project Director
David A. Munro

Consultant Editors
Martin W. Holdgate
John Burke

Executive Editor
Robin Rees

Commissioning Editor
William Hemsley

Copy editor
Emma Callery

Caption editor
Clint Twist

Proofreading
Frederika Straddling

Indexing
Ann Barret

Art Editor
Iona McGlashan

Art Director
Andrew Sutterby

Picture Research
Caroline Hensman

Production
Chris Latcham

First published in Great Britain in 1993 by Mitchell Beazley
an imprint of Reed Consumer Books Limited
Michelin House, 81 Fulham Road, London SW3 6RB
and Auckland, Melbourne, Singapore and Toronto

Copyright © Reed International Books Ltd, 1993

ISBN 1 85732 168 5

A CIP catalogue record for this book is available
at the British Library.

Reproduction by Alphabetset, London
Produced by Mandarin Offset, Hong Kong
Printed and bound in Hong Kong

Dollars ($): To aid comparisons, most sums of money are
given in United States Dollars (their value being that at time
of going to press).
Billions: The usage of the word billion varies, but in all cases here
it refers to thousand millions (1,000 million = 1 billion).

Half-title page picture: Blessing the first harvest of corn, Peru.
Title page picture: Trees in Yellowstone Park, United States.

Contents

This book is a popular adaptation of *Caring for the Earth: A Strategy for Sustainable Living,* which was published by IUCN – The World Conservation Union, UNEP (United Nations Environment Programme) and WWF (World Wide Fund For Nature) in 1991. The parent volume is a more detailed presentation of the same message. Both of these books are successors to the *World Conservation Strategy,* published by the same organizations in 1980.

Foreword

This book presents a strategy for a kind of development that provides real improvements in the quality of human life and at the same time conserves the vitality and diversity of the Earth. The goal is development that meets these needs in a sustainable way. Today it may seem visionary, but it is attainable. To more and more people it also appears our only rational option.

Most current development fails because it meets human needs incompletely and often destroys or degrades its resource base. We need development that is both people-centred, concentrating on improving the human condition, and conservation-based, maintaining the variety and productivity of nature. We have to stop talking about conservation and development as if they were in opposition, and recognize that they are essential parts of one indispensable process.

Caring for the Earth sets out a broad and explicit world strategy for the changes needed to build a sustainable society. We need such a strategy because:
• The most important issues we face are strongly interlinked, and therefore our actions must be mutually supportive and aimed at a common goal;
• The changes we must make in the ways in which we live and develop will be fundamental and far-reaching: they will demand our full dedication. The task will be easier if we work together;
• No single group can succeed by acting alone.

Any strategy has to be a guide rather than a prescription. It cannot be followed slavishly. Human societies differ greatly in culture, history, religion, politics, institutions and traditions. They also differ importantly in wealth, quality of life and environmental conditions, and in their awareness of the significance of these differences. Nor are these features fixed in time: change is continual. For these reasons, principles and actions are described in broad terms. They are meant to be interpreted and adapted by each community. The world needs a variety of sustainable societies, achieved by many different paths.

Martin W. Holdgate, Director General, IUCN

Elizabeth Dowdeswell, Executive Director, UNEP

Charles de Haes, Director General, WWF

Left A beautiful rainforest scene, Cross River State, Nigeria.

This first part is an introduction to the problems and challenges that we face now and will encounter in the future in caring for our planet and all of its inhabitants. It also introduces some fundamental ideas – such as those of sustainability and carrying capacity – and points to the need to modify our attitudes and activities. If we want to ensure a satisfactory life for all of us and for our descendants, we need to look closely at the ways we live, identify unwise activities and act to change them.

Left Refugees from war and famine at the Gaff Gaduud feeding centre, Somalia.

Gambling with Survival

The Earth and its resources are under pressure, and the strain is increasing. Huge numbers of people are made miserable by poverty. Many are struggling to survive. There is, however, no room for despair. To lessen suffering and the risk of environmental crises, development must take a new direction. People and society can make progress while still caring for the Earth.

This book has three central messages. The first is that if we, the world's people, want to ensure a satisfactory life for all of us and our descendants, we need a new kind of development. We must look at the ways we live and our activities; we must identify unwise practices and change them.

The second is that we depend on the Earth's resources for our basic and vital needs; if they are diminished or deteriorate, we run the risk that our needs and those of our descendants will not be met. Because we have been failing to care for the Earth, that risk has become dangerously great. We are now gambling with the future of civilization.

The third message is that we need not gamble. We can reduce the risk by ensuring that the benefits of development are distributed equitably, by learning to care for the Earth and by learning to live sustainably. We can change.

The capacity of the Earth

The lives of all of us are intimately tied to the resources our planet provides – resources such as air, water, soil, minerals, plants and animals. The extent of human impact on the Earth depends on the number of people there are and on how much of these resources each person uses. The maximum use of resources that the planet or a particular region can sustain defines its carrying capacity.

Above left Vast amounts of pollution in the form of smoke and fumes from the chimneys of factories and power stations pour into the atmosphere every year. The effects are many, depending on the substances that are emitted, and include deadly smogs, acid rain and even modifications in the climate of the Earth.

Left The Smokey Mountain slum area of Manila in the Philippines. Such great poverty is often the direct result of an increasing population that overstretches the economic resources of a region. While economic resources can be expanded, this must not be done at the expense of damage to natural resources, if long-term benefit is to result.

Carrying capacity can be increased by agriculture
and technology, but usually at the cost of reducing
biological diversity or of disrupting ecological
processes. In any case, it is not infinitely expand-
able. It is limited ultimately by nature's ability to
replenish itself or to absorb wastes safely. Our civ-
ilizations are now at risk because we are misusing
resources and disturbing natural systems. We are
pressing the Earth to the limits of its capacity.

Since the beginning of the industrial age in the
1700s, human numbers have grown eight-fold.
The 5.5 billion people now on Earth are using in
one way or another at least 40 per cent of our
most fundamental resource – the energy from the
Sun made available by plants on land. Industrial
production has risen by more than 100 times in
the past 100 years, and over the last two centuries
water withdrawals have grown from 100 to 3,600
cubic kilometres (24 to 864 cubic miles) per year.

This increase in human numbers and activity
has had an enormous impact on the environment.
The diversity of life on Earth has diminished. In
less than 200 years, the planet has lost 6 million
square kilometres (2.3 million square miles) of forest. So much soil is stripped away by erosion that
the volume of sediment in rivers has risen three-
fold in major river basins and by eight times in

We are pressing
the Earth to the limits of
its capacity

smaller, more intensively used ones. Atmospheric
systems have been disturbed, threatening the climate pattern to which we and other forms of life
are accustomed. Pollution has entered our air, soil
and water, including the oceans, and has become
an increasingly widespread threat to health.

Despite this vast take-over of nature, hundreds
of millions of people struggle in poverty, lacking a
tolerable quality of life. One person in five cannot
get enough food to support an active working life.
Every year millions die from malnutrition and preventable diseases. Such conditions are not only
grossly unjust, but threaten the peace and stability
of many countries, and ultimately of the world.

Tropical Forest

Arable Land

Human Population

1980

2000

2020

Above If current rates of land degradation continue, as much as one third of the arable land that existed in 1980 will be unproductive by 2000; over the same period, the area of unlogged tropical forest will have halved and human population will have increased by almost half. The third graph shows what will happen if these rates of change continue to 2020.

Above right Burning rubbish and rusting discarded vehicles on a landfill site mar the beauty of the landscape. Excessive production of waste is often symptomatic of unnecessary, excessive or wasteful consumption. In the higher-income countries, enormous amounts are discarded by each person.

Unless death rates rise sharply, the global human population seems certain to reach at least 10 billion. It may reach 12 billion. If so many people suffer from an inadequate quality of life now, how will billions more be able to find the food, water, health care and shelter they need? How can this vast increase in human numbers be supported without irreversible damage to the Earth? Clearly not by our continuing to live as we do now; clearly not by a policy of business as usual. Instead we have to find new ways to live and develop – ways that conserve Earth's vitality and are therefore sustainable in the long term.

Foundations for change

The change to living sustainably and caring for the Earth will be a major one for most people. We must stop talking about conservation and development as if they were in opposition, and recognize that they are parts of one indispensable process.

Living sustainably must become a principle for everybody, but it never will be while hundreds of millions survive without even the essentials of a good life. To make it possible for us all to think of the welfare of later generations – and other species – we need a new kind of development that rapidly improves the quality of life for the disadvantaged. For humanity to develop on a sustainable basis will be impossible unless both human population and the demand for resources level off within the carrying capacity of the Earth. We should try to leave a substantial safety margin between our total impact on the Earth and our estimate of what the environment can withstand. This is all the more important because, while we know that ultimate limits exist, we are uncertain as to what the limits are and at exactly what point we may reach them. To keep within the limits of what the Earth can safely support and to see that those people who now have least can soon get more, two major changes are essential. First, population growth must level off in all parts of the world and, second, the rich must stabilize, and in some cases reduce, their consumption of resources.

The goal of development that meets human needs in a sustainable way may seem visionary today, but it is attainable. To more and more people it also appears our only rational option.

Ultimately, we must take no more from nature than nature can replenish. This means adopting lifestyles and development paths that work within nature's limits. Sustainability can be achieved without sacrificing the many benefits that modern technology has brought, provided that technology also works within those limits. We need a new approach to the future, not a return to the past.

We have to stop talking about conservation and development as if they were always in opposition

Any strategy has to be a guide rather than a prescription. Human societies differ greatly in culture, history, religion, politics, institutions and traditions. They also differ importantly in wealth, quality of life and environmental conditions, and in their awareness of these differences. Moreover, these features are not fixed in time, for change is continual. The appropriate steps towards a sustainable future depend on local circumstances. The world needs a variety of sustainable societies, achieved by many different paths.

Whatever paths we chose, we need to understand and accept the consequences of being part of the great community of life and to become more conscious of the effects of our decisions on other societies, future generations and other species. We need to plan what we do on an ethical basis.

What does "sustainability" mean?

If an activity is "sustainable", for all practical purposes it can continue forever. Carrying out an activity sustainably now will not jeopardize the same activity in the future. Sustainability can have biological, environmental, economic and social dimensions. All are important.

Whaling, for example, has been notoriously unsustainable, all but wiping out its own future by running down the stocks of one species after another to the point where more hunting became unprofitable. But any fishing industry can be sustainable in biological terms if the annual catch is not too great for the remaining fish to rebuild their population each year. It can be sustainable in economic terms so long as the price received for the fish is not less than the cost of catching them. It can be sustainable in social terms so long as the fisher folk are satisfied with the conditions of their lives. Finally, even if all these conditions are met, the fishery would not be sustainable for environmental reasons if the fish population declined because of pollution.

The concept of sustainability also applies in a wider environmental sense. In this respect a sustainable society is one that does not jeopardize the air, water, soil, and plant and animal life on which our well-being depends.

"Sustainable development", therefore, refers to improving the quality of human life while at the same time living within the carrying capacity of supporting ecosystems.

A "sustainable economy", in turn, is the product of sustainable development. It maintains its natural resource base, but it can develop by adapting and by improvements in knowledge, organization, technical efficiency and, not least, wisdom. "Sustainability" cannot, on the other hand, refer to growth that continues to use more raw materials or yield an increasing volume of products. Nothing physical can grow indefinitely.

Judging whether an activity is truly sustainable is rarely straightforward, not only because of the complexity of the decision, but also because circumstances can change unexpectedly. When an activity is defined as being sustainable, it is on the basis of what is known at the time. Judgements must be made based on the best knowledge that is available. There can not be any long-term guarantee of sustainability, however, because errors may have been made or knowledge may have been inadequate. The moral we may draw is: be conservative in actions that could affect the environment, study the effects of such actions carefully and learn quickly from any mistakes.

Left Construction of houses by masons trained in new techniques. The houses are of traditional design, in keeping with local custom and culture. The new methods, however, avoid using the locally scarce wood that is employed by traditional construction methods.

Above A "biogaz" machine, operated at Karjat, near Bombay, India. It uses waste plant matter to generate gas that can then be used as a fuel, thus saving precious wood. The plant matter that is used will grow again for next season's harvest, and so is a sustainable resource.

Ethics and the Community of Life

Ethics asks the questions: how should we live and what moral principles should guide our conduct? Ethics in relation to the environment and human development asks the more specific question: how should we act towards the Earth and the whole community of life that shares this planet?

To stress that we have a duty of care and respect for people and other forms of life is to express an ethical belief. It holds that development should not be at the expense of other groups or later generations, that we should share fairly the benefits and costs of the use of resources and of conservation, that we have a responsibility to all life, and that nature must be cared for in its own right, not just to satisfy human needs.

The idea that ethics can illuminate the relationship between people and nature goes back thousands of years, forming part of many cultures and a significant element in the major religions. Many religions and moral philosophies remind us of the unity of the community of life and stress the importance of our stewardship of nature.

Above An Afghani farmer prays in a wheat field. Islam requires that believers pray at set times each day, wherever they are. By not emphasizing the actual place where worship takes place, Islam acknowledges the links between religious belief and the living planet. Islamic teaching states that all living creatures are worthy of our respect and that we were entrusted with the Earth by God; thus it is our duty to care for our planet.

Above Inside a village hut in Cameroon an elder of the Leopard Cult sits with spiritually charged leaves. The belief that all plants and animals, including humans, are imbued with the same spiritual forces, if with varying degrees of power, is widespread among the traditional cultures of many indigenous peoples.

Left A Buddhist monk in Thailand waters a young sapling. The sapling, along with thousands of others, will be transplanted to the wild as part of the attempt to repair Thailand's deforested hillsides. The reafforestation programme has become a national priority, and is in accord with the Buddhist conception of life.

Patterns of belief

Indigenous people in many places attribute supernatural powers and sentience to plants and animals, and to the Sun, the Moon, the winds and the sea. Such people respect other forms of life, even those they hunt. The land itself is considered to be worthy of respect and can not be possessed by individuals. It was for the use of everyone, in the same way as the air and the sea – a belief still held by many traditional cultures.

The more formalized faiths also address the ethical dimension of human relationships with nature. Hinduism and Buddhism, the major religions of the East, differ from their Western counterparts in their views of time and the processes of life. Hinduism considers time to be cyclical, reflecting the interdependent rise, maturation and fall of all that exists. Each life, whatever its form, has a soul which moves from one being when it dies to another. This belief has powerful implications for the attitude people should take to all forms of life. As Karan Singh, a Hindu scholar, has put it:

The Hindu viewpoint on nature ... is permeated by a reverence for life, and an awareness that the great forces of nature – the earth, the sky, the air, the water and the fire – as well as various orders of life, including plants and trees, forests and animals, are all bound to each other within the great rhythms of nature.

Buddhism embodies a similar set of concepts to those of Hinduism concerning the cyclical and interdependent nature of life. The respect for nature that is inherent in Buddhism is reflected in such things as sacred forests and sacred mountains, and in the natural sanctuaries that surround many Buddhist monasteries.

Unlike the faiths that take a cyclical view of the passage of life and time, Judaism holds that time is linear and sequential. It moves from beginning to end, and each life is lived only once. Judaism emphasizes the existence of a living God and the need for humankind, which is the final and greatest creation of God, to accept a responsibility to care for the rest of God's creatures. Rabbi Arthur Herzberg, vice-president of the World Jewish Congress, has said:

The rebirth of nature, day after day, is God's gift but humanity is the custodian of this capacity of the Earth to renew itself. As we consume any one of the products of divine bounty, we must first say the appropriate grace. The world is His and we are but sojourners. At the very least we must leave the palace of our Host no worse than we found it.

We have a duty of care and respect for all people and other forms of life

Christian belief in the life, death and resurrection of Christ implies the sinfulness of humanity but also the possibility of future salvation. Christians believe that they can become instruments of the will of God for all of his creation. Christian interpretation of the relationship between people and other life – from Medieval times through until quite recently – was seen as one of human dominance and control over nature. Now, however, the role of humankind as a steward of God's creation is being reasserted.

In Islam it is also the linear view of time and the supremacy of humanity as the vice-regent of Allah that shapes ethics. Conservation of the environment is based on the principle that each one of its components was created by God, each having a different function measured and balanced by the Creator. Human use is only one of the reasons for the creation of all the many parts of the natural world; other creatures are also beings worthy of respect. The environment is the gift of God to all ages, past, present and future, and God entrusted humans with the duty of protecting it.

Conservation and environmental ethics

Modern conservation has drawn on ethical philosophies that stress both intrinsic and instrumental (practical) values for the natural world. Wilderness enthusiasts and animal-rights advocates stress intrinsic values; resource conservationists stress instrumental values for human welfare. The notion of conservation as it has developed over the last 100 years has drawn on values that include a duty of care for both nature and people. In the 1930s, Aldo Leopold proposed a land ethic that:

reflects the existence of an ecological conscience, and this in turn reflects a conviction of individual responsibility for the health of the land.

Such ethics have long been overshadowed, most potently by the Western utilitarian view, which was a product of the scientific and industrial revolutions of the seventeenth and eighteenth centuries. In essence, Earth's resources were seen as being there for the taking. In recent decades, however, there has been an increasing effort to restate an ethical approach appropriate to modern times.

Building world ethics for living sustainably

An ethical framework for sustainable living – a set of consistent and morally compelling principles that could guide all peoples of the world – has been proposed (see box opposite). It is founded on a belief in people as a creative force, and in the value of every human individual and each human society. It can be implemented within the cultural context of each society. The framework recognizes the need to improve the quality of human life and remove inequalities, while stressing the respect and care we owe not just to each other but to all forms of life on Earth. It provides an ethical basis for the ideas and actions proposed in this book.

An ethical framework is important because what people do depends on what they believe. Widely shared beliefs are often more powerful than government edicts. The transition to sustainable societies will require changes in how we perceive one another, other life, the Earth, and our needs and priorities. People in many societies need to change their attitudes towards nature because it can no longer meet their demands or withstand their impacts. We have a right to nature's benefits, but we must recognize that these will not be available unless we care for nature as well.

Bottom left Protesters at an anti-whaling rally in Glasgow, Scotland. During the 1980s, the campaign to save the great whales successfully mobilized international public opinion against the killing of great whales. Such campaigns can bring together people with a wide range of ethical backgrounds to express a common belief.

No major society yet lives by a value system that gives proper regard to the future of human communities and other life. Without one, however, a satisfactory human future is in jeopardy: poverty, strife and tragedy are certain to increase, and few will escape their influence. Individual actions are, perhaps for the first time, combining to cause global problems. The ethical principles enabling us to resolve them must be agreed worldwide.

The establishment of world ethics needs the support of the world's religions because they have spoken for centuries about the individual's duty of care for fellow humans and of reverence for divine creation. It also needs the backing of those non-religious groups that are concerned with the principles that should govern relationships among people, and with nature.

> **Individual actions are, perhaps for the first time, combining to cause global problems**

Respect for other forms of life is easiest in those cultures and societies that emphasize that humanity is both apart from and a part of nature. It is most evident in those communities whose lives are lived in close contact with nature, and whose traditions of care for nature endure. This is the basis of the special contribution that indigenous peoples can make to the rediscovery of sustainable living by the world community.

Above Refugees from drought at the Las Dure camp in Somalia fetch water from a well that has been scraped in the desert sand. If people around the world continue to live unsustainably, disasters such as that which occurred in Somalia will only increase in number and frequency.

Left The Bom Futura tin mine in Brazil, carved out of the living rainforest. As ores are sought in increasingly more environmentally sensitive locations, it is our responsibility to future generations to minimize environmental damage and loss of resources.

Elements of world ethics for living sustainably

• Every human being is a part of the community of life, which is made up of all living creatures. This community links all human societies, present and future generations, and humanity and all other parts of nature. It embraces both cultural and natural diversity.

• Every human being has the same fundamental and equal rights, including the rights to: life, liberty and security; freedom of thought, conscience and religion; freedom of enquiry and expression; peaceful assembly and association; participation in government; education; and, within the limits of the Earth, to the resources needed for a decent standard of living. No individual, community or nation has the right to deprive another of its means of subsistence.

• Each person and each society is entitled to the respect of these rights; and is responsible for the protection of these rights for all others.

• Every life form warrants respect, independently of its value to people. Human development should not threaten the integrity of nature or the survival of other species. People should treat all creatures decently, and protect them from cruelty, avoidable suffering and unnecessary killing.

• All people should take responsibility for their impacts on nature. People should conserve ecological processes and natural diversity, and use resources frugally and efficiently, ensuring that their uses of renewable resources are sustainable.

• Everyone should aim to share fairly the benefits and costs of resources used among communities and groups, among regions that are poor and those that are affluent, and between present and future generations. Each generation should leave a world that is as diverse and productive as the one it inherited. Development of one society or generation should not limit the opportunities of others.

Above Participants in a marine ecology course in Kenya study a mangrove thicket, one of the most productive of all ecosytems, and often highly threatened. The ethical awareness that arises from the study of ecology and associated issues should not be confined to ecologists. People are able to take proper responsibility for their actions only if they understand the consequences of what they do.

Spreading the word

Winning support for the ethical framework for living sustainably requires action on a broad front. It is not enough to publicize the new approach, because even well-informed people do not necessarily take the right decisions. Because values determine how people pursue their political, legal, economic or technological goals, ethical values must pervade all spheres of human action if they are to succeed in their goals.

Effective implementation of the framework means that every one of us must take up its ideas and spread the message in various ways. It needs parents and educators to teach respect for other people and other species, while, in turn, school pupils and students can spread the new ideas they have learned. Artists can use their creative skills to inspire people with a understanding and respect for nature. Scientists can contribute by studying ecosystems, their sensitivity and their capacity to meet human needs, and by ensuring that their findings are communicated accurately and applied responsibly. Lawyers can evaluate the legal implications of the framework for world ethics and draft laws to support it.

Technologists, economists and industrialists should establish new ethically based approaches that implement the ideas expressed in the ethical framework. Politicians, policy makers and public administrators should work in a similar way to evaluate the changes that are needed in public policy, and then to put them into effect. Governments should incorporate the principles of ethics for living sustainably into their national legislations or their constitutions. Internationally, politicians should adopt a covenant that commits states to a world ethic for living sustainably and defines their rights and responsibilities accordingly.

Continuing development

Although the broad philosophy for an ethic for living sustainably is clear, the process of extending and clarifying the principles – including discussion of how to apply them – is only just beginning and requires the fullest possible participation. There needs to be continuing dialogue between all sectors of society, particularly representatives from religion, politics, moral philosophy, writers concerned with human conduct, and organizations concerned with the environment.

All people can become involved in developing ethics through discussion

All people can become involved in developing ethics through discussion in religious and citizens' groups and in environmental or humanitarian associations. Major religions should continue to identify and discuss the elements of their faiths that establish a duty of care for nature. Coalitions of organizations concerned with respecting and caring for the community of life could be formed nationally, and linked by international networks. Existing partnerships, such as the World Wide Fund For Nature's Network on Conservation and Religion and IUCN – The World Conservation Union's Ethics Working Group, could be brought within this framework.

Further development of ethics will clarify the relationships between human obligations, human rights and the rights of nature, and help to resolve any conflicts of interest (see box on this page).

Above **In a Cameroon school yard, children finish a mural that celebrates the colour and vitality of the countryside. An early appreciation of the variety and harmony of life helps to instil a sense of the value of the environment, not least as something of beauty that can give great pleasure.**

Right **A hunter with a seal taken from Lake Baikal in Siberia. In certain cases, conservation laws need to take into account the traditional subsistence hunting rights of indigenous peoples. This often involves balancing pragmatic reasons against ethical principles.**

Conflicts of interest

The obligation to respect every species regardless of its value to people may conflict with human interests if a species endangers human health or survival. Most people feel that it is morally justifiable to eradicate a human pathogen that is responsible for considerable loss of human lives, poor health and disability. Such species include human immunodeficiency viruses (HIV), smallpox virus, poliomyelitis virus, *Plasmodium falciparum* (which causes malaria) and Guinea worm.

However, it can be argued that, while control of harmful species may be justified, in no case is it right to seek the extinction of a species. Perhaps we should keep the last surviving pathogens in internationally controlled laboratories, as has happened with the smallpox virus.

The obligation to protect all creatures from cruelty and avoidable suffering can also conflict with the requirement that no people should be deprived of their means of subsistence. The campaign against the fur trade has deprived indigenous people in Greenland and northern Canada of a major source of income – for some communities, the only source – even though they were harvesting those resources sustainably.

Ethical principles need to be developed to resolve these dilemmas.

Conserving Earth's Vitality

The thin outer layer of our planet in which we and all other life exists is called the "biosphere". It includes the land, the seas and the atmosphere; it consists of the community of life and all the non-living parts of the planet that contain, support and sustain life. We, like all other organisms, are dependent on the biosphere for our survival and are an integral part of it.

The biosphere is a great interdependent system. All its components interact to influence one another and the whole. "Ecosystems" function in the same way, but on a smaller scale. An ecosystem is any interacting set of plants, animals and other organisms combined with the non-living components of their environment, such as soil, water and air. We can, for example, talk of a forest ecosystem or a grassland ecosystem. The biosphere, in effect, is a vast set of interlocking, functioning ecosystems.

The biosphere is supplied with light and heat energy from the Sun. Green plants perform the key function in ecosystems: they are the site of photosynthesis and so are life's basic producers – sometimes known as primary producers. Using carbon dioxide from the air, water, nutrients drawn from the soil and the energy of sunlight, they manufacture sugars, starches, oils and proteins. These are the substances that from the building blocks for everything that we call food.

All other life depends either directly or indirectly on plants. Many animals graze or browse on them, or eat their seeds or fruits. Others prey upon the plant eaters. The cycle is completed by decomposers, including many insects, worms, protozoa, fungi and bacteria, that break down wastes and dead remains to release the nutrients.

As well as the interdependencies among plants and animals, the quality, quantity and distribution of water and soil, as well as air quality, are highly important factors in the functioning of living systems. All can be subject to change.

Ecosystems are dynamic; they can often adapt to change so long as it is not too rapid or profound. However, they can be damaged, sometimes seriously; for example, if trees are cut faster than they can replace themselves, pastures are grazed too heavily, soil is allowed to be eroded, water is polluted, or a species is exterminated.

Today, human disturbance of ecosystems has become a worldwide problem. The biosphere is increasingly dominated by our behaviour in ways that are putting species and habitats at risk, upsetting ecological processes, damaging resources and ultimately threatening our own well-being.

Lifeforms under siege

Plants and animals, associated in ecosystems and evolving over hundreds of millions of years have made the planet fit for the myriad forms of life we know today. They help to maintain the chemical balance of the Earth and to stabilize the climate.

Prudence dictates that we keep as much of the variety of life as possible. Natural diversity is, however, more threatened today than at any other time since the extinction of the dinosaurs 65 million years ago. The situation is likely to become steadily worse as more and more wild habitats are converted for human uses, destroying the homes of animals and plants. Alteration of a habitat can render it just as unsuitable for wildlife – too many livestock kept on natural pasture, for example, can thin out the vegetation too much for the needs of wild herbivores. Pollution released into air and water directly poisons some creatures. Hunting and capture are severe threats to many wildlife populations, especially those that have already dwindled because of habitat changes. The accidental or deliberate release of non-native species into ecosystems where local species are not adapted to cope with them is a further threat. For example, rats from ships are a problem for many isolated island ecosystems. The introduced species, through excessive predation, competition for space, light or food, or the transmission of parasites and disease, can cause native species to die out.

We are still uncertain about how many species exist, and estimates vary considerably. However, some experts calculate that, if present trends continue, up to 25 per cent of the world's species could become extinct, or be reduced to tiny remnants, by the middle of the next century.

Top left **Life behind bars. An illegally imported blue-and-yellow macaw in its cage at a rescue centre in the Netherlands. The illegal (and sometimes legal) import of animals as pets and of plants as decoration is threatening a number of endangered species around the world.**

Left Red mangroves overhang a shallow-water coral reef in Belize. Ecosystems based on mangroves and corals are species-rich and highly productive, but they can easily be severely damaged by even moderate levels of marine pollution.

Below A Kenyan wildlife ranger sits among a selection of confiscated animal items seized in Nairobi. Poaching, often spurred on by markets in the higher-income countries, is a severe threat to many endangered species.

Despoiling nature

The pressures on wild plants and animals are undermining the health and productivity of many ecosystems. There are also severe problems on a global scale. For example, greenhouse gases, produced mainly by people burning fossil fuels, clearing forests and raising crops and livestock, accumulate in the atmosphere increasing its heat-trapping properties and so raise global temperature. The shield of stratospheric ozone is being depleted, mainly by chlorofluorocarbons (CFCs) – from such things as aerosol cannisters – letting through harmful ultra-violet rays from the Sun.

At the same time, old pollution problems that once were local in scale now affect large regions. Over much of Europe and North America acid deposition (in rain, mist and snow) pollutes water, acidifies soils, kills trees and corrodes buildings.

Old pollution problems that once were local in scale now affect large regions

The natural world is despoiled in other ways too. For example, pollution is only one of the factors that threaten the productivity and diversity of surface waters, such as rivers and lakes. The forms of river beds, the speed and pattern of water flow, quantity and distribution of aquatic plant and animal life have been disrupted time and again by the damming and channelling of streams, and the dredging and drainage of wetlands. Coastal ecosystems are deteriorating because of mounting human pressure, including urban and tourist development along shores, shipping, poorly regulated fish-farming and uncontrolled waste disposal.

Right Scarcely recognizable as the living creature it once was, an oil-soaked cormorant is washed ashore on a tide of oil in Saudi Arabia. During the Gulf War of 1990–91, the world was shocked by the use of mass-pollution – in the form of oil released into the sea – as a weapon of war.

Overexploitation

The resources that we use fall into two distinct categories: those that are renewable and those that are non-renewable. Renewable resources are those that we can continue using without them running out, either because they recycle quite rapidly (for example, water) or because they can replace themselves or be propagated quite quickly (for example, plants and animals).

Non-renewable resources are those whose consumption necessarily involves their depletion. Minerals are non-renewable and, effectively, so are oil, gas and coal. It takes millions of years for these resources to form. The more of them we use, the less is available for the future.

Renewable resources are the base of all economies. People cannot live without them. They include soil and water, the products we harvest from the wild (such as timber, nuts, medicinal plants, fish and the meat and skins of wild animals), the domesticated species raised by farmers, and ecosystems (such as rangelands, forests and waters). If used sustainably, such resources will perpetually renew themselves.

Because much of the fishing, wood-cutting and grazing carried out at present is not sustainable, the future of many human communities is threatened. For instance, overfishing combined with natural fluctuations in numbers of fish has caused the decline of some fisheries and greater instability in others. Most fisheries are exploited beyond levels that are likely to be sustainable in the long term. Woodlands in many regions have been severely depleted because of cutting for fuelwood; now some rural areas face a severe fuel crisis. Overused pasture, denuded of protective vegetation by excessive grazing and trampling, makes up much of the agricultural land that is rendered unproductive each year by soil erosion.

Conservation imperatives

As is all too clear, conservation of nature is essential for sustainable development and the future of humanity. Further, it is a matter of ethics as well as practicality to manage development so that it does not threaten the survival of other species or eliminate their habitats. Concerted action is needed to reverse our destructive trends and to protect the structure, functions and diversity of the world's natural systems on which our species utterly depends. This requires us to conserve biodiversity, conserve life-support systems and ensure that uses of renewable resources are sustainable.

Biodiversity is the total variety of all genetic strains, species and ecosystems on the planet. In order to preserve as much biodiversity as possible, it is important to safeguard not just vulnerable or endangered species, by protecting them against exploitation and unnatural hazards, but entire ecosystems, through the establishment of specific protected areas and by wider-ranging conservation measures to protect the range of habitats within the countryside as a whole.

Life-support systems are the ecological processes that shape climate, cleanse air and water, regulate water flow, recycle nutrients, create and regenerate soil, and keep the planet fit for life. To relieve the strain on life-support systems, action is urgently needed to reduce human impact on ecosystems. Pollution emissions can be reduced by a mixture of improved technology, better management of waste, more sparing use of hazardous materials and a switch to alternatives, demanded by regulations or promoted by fiscal measures.

Below A Turkana nomad drives his goats through a desiccated and overgrazed landscape in northern Kenya. Goats have considerable economic importance because they can graze successfully on poor pasture, but this success contains the seeds of destruction. Goats can severely overgraze vulnerable land.

Right Women unloading firewood in the highlands of Ecuador. Millions of people rely on wood as their only or main source of fuel, but increasing demands often result in more being taken than nature can replenish, leading to denuded landscapes. Fuelwood is a renewable resource, but only if properly managed.

Conserving natural ecosystems

Virtually no ecosystems in the world are entirely "natural" in the sense of having escaped all human influence. However, even if we define what a natural ecosystem is more realistically – as one where human impact has been no greater than that of any other species and has not affected the ecosystem's structure – we find that few remain in most upper-income countries or in densely populated areas of lower-income countries. Forests, wetlands, scrublands and grasslands are all giving way to agriculture and urban development. Such conversion is often undertaken to meet compelling human demands, and it will be difficult to halt when human populations and needs are increasing so greatly and so rapidly. However, many conversions of ecosystems are reducing biodiversity and productivity, and are demonstrably unsustainable.

Conservation of nature is essential for the future of humanity

Human activities need to be managed in an integrated way so that they do not cause unneccesary loss of natural ecosystems, do not cause disruption downstream or on adjacent sites, do not reduce the productivity of farmlands, forests or fisheries, and protect such things as soil, ground cover and water resources.

Uses of a renewable resource must be kept within its capacity for renewal. Achieving this depends on better knowledge and understanding of the long-term capacity for exploitation without depletion, and better management to keep within this capacity. Research and the monitoring of stocks to increase knowledge and understanding should be given high priority. Management should have two thrusts: on the one hand, careful regulation of harvesting levels, and on the other, education and economic incentives aimed at motivating resource users to conserve and maintain the stocks on which their livelihoods depend.

Above **Drums of fuel being moved in Antarctica, the closest thing that we have to a pristine environment. International regulations state that all waste must be removed from the continent, but localized pollution and disturbance are still caused by human activity.**

Striking the correct balance between alternative uses of the environment is the most difficult task that faces conservation and development planners today. Sustainability depends on converting to human use only those areas that will be able to support the usage that is under consideration. At the same time natural ecosystems should be retained where they provide the greatest benefits or are essential in maintaining biodiversity and ecological functions. Great care is needed in land-use decisions because, once land has been converted to cultivation or other uses, restoration to a diverse natural system, such as a mature forest, can take centuries.

Working Together for Change

How people manage their lives and the ways governments and businesses act affect everyone's ability to live sustainably. These factors also affect international relations, including conditions of and developments in trade and financial flows. Changes in attitudes, life styles, government and international relations are needed to make it easier for societies to turn good ideas into actions.

Our goal must be a new kind of development, one centred on people and based on conservation, concentrating on improving the quality of life for all and maintaining the variety and productivity of nature. Achieving such a goal requires actions in many fields. However, carrying out new ideas will be difficult unless we also make changes in the ways we, personally and collectively, make decisions and organize our activities. More often than not it is a matter of priorities. Sustainable living must become the key to the way in which humans operate at all levels – individuals, communities, nations and the world community.

Attitudes and life styles

There are many reasons why people live unsustainably. Poverty, for example, can force people to do things that will help them to survive for the present, even though they know they are creating problems for the future. Desperate efforts to escape from poverty, perhaps by raising crops on slopes that are too steep, may only make matters worse in the longer term. Yields drop and the environment becomes further degraded.

In many lower-income countries, the first priority must therefore be to increase people's earnings and build the infrastructure – the health care, social services, housing and other support – that will give people more secure livelihoods and a firm foundation for adopting the practices that are necessary for living sustainably.

The rich may live unsustainably because of ignorance or lack of concern, and because wasteful consumption is often promoted by advertising and marketing strategies. For them, particularly, the need is to change attitudes and practices. To adopt an ethic for living sustainably, people must examine their values and alter their behaviour. Affluent societies must promote values that support new ethics and discourage those that are incompatible with sustainable living. This is essential, not only so that resources are used more sustainably, but also to bring about the changes in international economic, trade and aid policies and practices that can help other societies to live more sustainably.

People in different countries have to alter their life styles in different ways. But despite these differences, there is a widespread need to prepare people for changes that are likely to conflict with their accepted values. Education and training, as well as campaigning, will be an important part of preparing people for such changes.

There is a base to build on. Various opinion polls suggest that concern about environmental deterioration is common in all countries. Many people are voicing demands to protect nature and to show responsibility for future generations. However, other surveys show that people quickly tire if all they hear are messages of doom, and even those who accept the need to live differently often fail to follow their ideals. Despite widespread concern for environmental issues in many high-income countries, for instance, not enough people adopt a driving style that conserves energy, recycle their domestic waste or place environmental friendliness above convenience when shopping.

Attitude surveys also show that the links between individual life styles, the alleviation of poverty, the use of resources, and world economic and trading patterns are not widely understood. Many people simply do not see how changing their own behaviour would help others. Accurate, understandable information must be disseminated and promoted so that the positive actions needed for the survival and well-being of the world's societies can be fully understood.

Above Schoolchildren show their support for protection of the African elephant at the 1989 CITES conference in Lusanne, Switzerland. There is much public concern about environmental issues, often particularly among young people. This concern, however, must be translated into the practice of sustainable living.

Right Omani children reading books about local wildlife. The government of Oman provides information to young people on a range of environmental issues. Education to bring about awareness of the environment is important if children are to grow up sufficiently informed to make their own decisions about sustainable living.

Caring communities

Care for the Earth and sustainable living may depend upon the beliefs and actions of individuals, but it is through their communities that most people can best express their commitment. People who organize themselves to work for sustainability in their own communities can be a powerful and effective force, whether their community is rich, poor, urban, suburban or rural.

At the same time, many of the problems of human development and environmental quality arise at the community level. In many parts of the world, land rights are not shared equitably, leaving some farmers with inadequate income or forcing them to farm marginal plots that rapidly become exhausted. The quality of people's water supply and of the air that they breathe depend largely on

**It is through their communities
that most people can
best express their commitment**

their community - on the provision of piped water and sewerage, the management of traffic and the location and practices of industry, and the respect of each inhabitant for the interests of others. Issues also arise concerning resources shared between communities. Persistent overfishing by one lakeside village, for example, depletes not just its own resource but that of neighbouring villages.

A sustainable community cares for all of its members and for its own environment, and does not damage the environments of others. It uses resources wisely, recycles materials, minimizes wastes and disposes of them safely, and conserves local ecosystems. It meets its own needs as far as it can, but recognizes the need to work in partnership with other communities.

To fully implement the change to sustainability, the community and all its members must have secure access to land and other natural resources. Local management of resources should be encouraged on a basis that involves every sector of the community. Community environmental action will not work unless all citizens have a right to participate in decisions that affect them.

Left and above In January 1993, the Braer oil tanker was wrecked in stormy weather off the Shetland Islands, United Kingdom, creating a huge oil slick. Although some experts classified the ecological damage as "minimal", volunteers had to collect thousands of oil-covered sea birds, many dead, from local beaches.

National frameworks

It is essential to build a public consensus around an ethic for living sustainably, and to encourage individuals and communities to take action. It is equally important, however, to ensure an effective national approach. For this purpose, governments must provide a national framework (and in federal countries, provincial or state frameworks as well) of institutions, economic policies, national laws and regulations that are all aimed at the creation of a sustainable society.

During the past two decades, many countries have established administrative departments and other institutions concerned with the environment. More than a hundred have established special agencies for environmental protection. However, many of these units have been added to existing bureaucracies, or set up with limited mandates and inadequate budgets. They have too often lacked the ability to enforce environmental protection and their initiatives often lie well down in the list of government priorities. Faced with recession or rising unemployment, for example, even environmentally aware governments are tempted to slacken pollution standards that would otherwise reduce the profitability of an existing industry or prevent a new industry from starting. For the main part,

environmental policy has been reactive, with governments responding to problems only after they have developed and when they are more expensive to treat than if they had been tackled early on.

Human impact on the environment is long term in its operation and complex in its causes and effects. It cannot be addressed in isolation with low-priority remedial, measures. The integration of human development and environmental conservation requires the establishment of institutions that are capable of a forward-looking and cross-sectoral approach to making decisions. Without such an approach, they are unlikely to develop effective policies and laws that safeguard human rights, the interests of future generations and the productivity and diversity of the Earth.

Laws affecting the environment provide essential back-up to the policies that are needed for sustainability. They protect and encourage the law-abiding, and guide citizens on the actions they should take. An important function of law is the application of sanctions to those who break it. No less important is its role in defining anti-social behaviour and discouraging people from acting in anti-social ways. Laws set standards, often forcing technological advances in the process, and mould public and administrative attitudes.

Full social cost

When industries assess the cost of their products, they conventionally take into account only the cost of production – the amounts they have to pay out for materials and labour, for processing and transportation. However, this is not a full reflection of their true cost.

The full social cost of a product is difficult to assess, but it must include environmental and user as well as production costs. Environmental cost refers to the wider implications of producing and using the product. It is the cost imposed on society through any damage to ecosystems and other resources as a result of degradation and pollution.

User cost is the value of future resources that is forgone because the resource stock has been reduced to supply the current product. It refers not only to non-renewable resources like oil and mineral ores, but also to renewable ones. If users of a forest, for example, alter the ecosystem so that it yields less than before they are reducing the future availability of timber.

Bottom A young Madagascan boy stands in the middle of a forest that has been cleared and burnt for cultivation – a practice that, unless very carefully managed, is highly unsustainable. Before the boy has reached the age of 30, the ground will probably be an infertile wasteland.

Below Air pollution around a smelting plant at Dillingen, Germany. Although Germany has relatively strict anti-pollution regulations, such measures are often ineffective without the support of adequate economic incentives. Such incentives should be based on the idea of "full social cost". As things stand, not only does the factory produce pollution, but the costs of its products (or of production) do not reflect the depletion of the non-renewable resources it consumes or of actually dealing with the pollution that it causes.

Without adequate economic incentives, however, policies and regulations are fighting an uphill battle. Every economy depends on the environment as a source of life-supporting services and raw materials. Conventional pricing systems do not take this into account, effectively treating most resources and the like as being limitless and the environment as free of charge (see box on this page). Because the cost of depleting resources and degrading ecosystems does not appear on the balance sheet, there is little incentive for industry to conserve them. However, new valuation methods that incorporate ethical, human and ecological costs as well as economic considerations are being developed. By using them, governments will be better able to apply taxes, charges and subsidies to resource users to discourage unsustainable practices and encourage those that are sustainable.

Policies and programmes for sustainability must be based on scientific knowledge of the factors that they will affect and by which they will be affected. Research that will improve understanding of the environment must continue. Equally, so must monitoring of changes in the environment because this is the most useful direct measure of the effectiveness of actions. Strengthening environmental research should be a national priority.

Acting globally

The environment links all nations. The atmosphere and the oceans interact to shape the world's climate. Climate change, ozone depletion and pollution of the air, rivers and seas have now become worldwide threats. Pollution knows no frontiers, because it drifts with currents of air and water. Environmental problems are becoming ever more international in scale.

Many national frontiers cut across natural systems such as river basins, estuaries, forests or range lands that are ecologically united. Many migratory species move across frontiers, and some travel between continents. Sustainability within a nation will thus be difficult to achieve unless there are international agreements in place to manage such cross-frontier resources.

Neither wealth nor sovereignty can protect us from these pervasive issues. The nations of the western Pacific, western Europe and North America – islands of wealth in an ocean of want – face a rising tide of migrants who are fleeing from environmental degradation and economic stagnation. These and other factors, from long-range weapons to modern communications and international money markets, are eroding the significance of national frontiers.

Yet many governments passionately defend the integrity of national frontiers, even though many are legacies of colonialism and make no ecological, ethnic or common sense. A key issue is whether frontiers will hold, be held by force, or crumble before a tide of environmental refugees. The only chance of stabilizing the situation lies in international co-operation on an unprecedented scale. States must stop regarding themselves as being self-sufficient units (which few, if any, are), and accept a future as components of a global system.

A global alliance requires acceptance by every nation of its share of responsibility, and a commitment by each nation to as much action as its means permit. Agreement must be reached on how to conserve global resources and to share the benefits derived from them equitably. Success will depend on effective, properly funded institutions, both non-governmental and intergovernmental, and the backing of international law. International co-operation that has already been achieved – for example, in the several conventions that help conserve biological diversity – must be strengthened and repeated on a much wider scale. The 1992 United Nations Conference on Environment and Development (UNCED), the Earth Summit in Rio de Janeiro, Brazil, helped to spread this message.

To increase the capacity of lower-income countries to support themselves, and in so doing to develop sustainably and protect their environments, their debts must be reduced and their terms of trade improved. Increased flows of finance are also essential, especially to Africa, Latin America and low-income Asia. This has yet to happen, however, because official development assistance has usually exported a style of managing people and resources that is inappropriate to the receivers. This style is now being seriously questioned but, so far, too much money has been held back to pay for consultants and equipment. Low-income countries need a different kind of assistance, one that helps them to build their own capacity to manage resources and develop sustainably.

Rich and poor are being prised ever further apart

Closing the gap

International relations must have at their heart the understanding that those nations with greater economic resources must contribute more to global well-being. At the same time, action must be taken to close the gap between rich and poor countries.

At present, rich and poor are being prised ever further apart. The Third World's cumulative debt, principally to Western governments and banks, is more than $1,000 billion. Interest payments on this sum alone have reached $60 billion a year. As a result, and despite aid programmes, there has been a net transfer of capital from lower-income to upper-income countries since 1984.

Most low-income countries obtain at least three-quarters of their export incomes from primary commodities. Prices of many of these, including copper, iron ore, sugar, rubber and timber, have fallen, undermining the economies of these countries. The prices, in any case, do not include the environmental and user costs of producing the resources. The natural wealth of the exporting countries is subsidizing the importers.

Meanwhile, political borders impede the flow of goods and services from the Third World. Trade barriers imposed by high-income countries cost lower-income countries two-and-a-half times more than all the aid they receive.

Left Members of the Kayapo tribe, who come from the Amazon rainforest, attending the opening of their exhibit at the 1992 Earth Summit in Brazil. The communication of local issues can help all groups and nations to understand and accept their share of responsibility for problems around the world.

Top Kurdish refugees reach the border between Iraq and Iran to escape persecution and the destruction of their means of livelihood. Political turmoil often results in ecological disasters and famine. Global co-operation is needed to deal with the many refugee problems that exist around the world.

Above On the Chicago Mercantile Exchange, traders speculate on the prices of commodities, much influenced by international trade conditions. If the price of a commodity, such as a crop, falls, traders can switch to another; but for farmers who grow that crop, the price fall may be a catastrophe.

Damage to the vitality and
diversity of nature, a rapidly
increasing population and the
demand for resources; poverty
and inadequate quality of life:
these are intimately related
issues that affect us all. The first
three chapters of this section
explore the problems and
identify actions to stabilize
population growth and moderate
consumption. The remaining
chapters go into further detail
about major areas of human
activity, and the supporting
ecosystems and natural resources.

Left Smoke rising from burning rainforest
beside the River Orinoco, Venezuela

Population and Resources

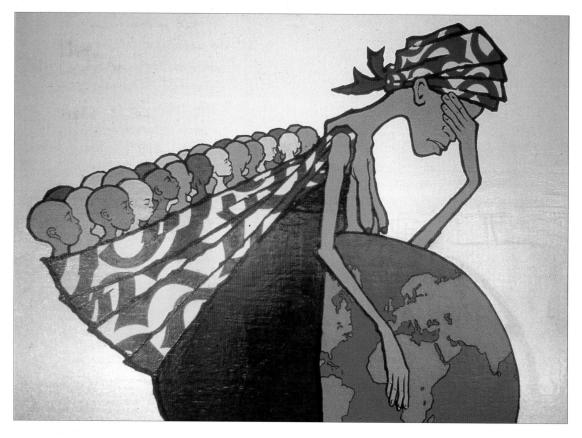

Ten thousand years ago, the total population of humans was probably something below 10 million. Most people lived by gathering wild food, inhabited simple dwellings and had scarcely any possessions. Since then human numbers have multiplied nearly 600 times and our demands on the planet's resources have changed drastically in both their manner and their scale. We use resources not only to meet our vast needs for food, shelter and energy, but also for a host of objects and processes, many relatively recently invented, that make our lives much easier and more comfortable than they ever were before.

The human population of the Earth started to rise several thousand years ago, when people first began to manage and improve some of the plants and animals they used as food. As supplies of food grew, so the land was able to support more and more people. By around 2,000 years ago, the world population had swollen to 250 million.

This rise took a further upward swing about 200 years ago following improvements in agriculture and great advances in manufacturing. This technological revolution began in Europe and went together with exploitation of overseas resources. Population rose sharply in Europe and later, as developments spread, throughout the world. Advances in health care played an enormous part, greatly lowering the death rate.

World population will reach 6.4 billion by the year 2000 and 10 billion by 2050

By 1900, world population was some 1.6 billion, and rising at an accelerating pace. In 1950, it was 2.5 billion. By 1987, it had doubled again. Today, the growth rate is starting to decline, but growth continues. The United Nations (UN) estimates that population will reach 6.4 billion by the year 2000 and, as a medium projection, 10 billion by 2050.

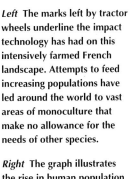

Left The marks left by tractor wheels underline the impact technology has had on this intensively farmed French landscape. Attempts to feed increasing populations have led around the world to vast areas of monoculture that make no allowance for the needs of other species.

Right The graph illustrates the rise in human population since 1750 and predicts the rise until 2050. The change in shape of the curve between the years 2000 and 2050 shows a reduction in the rate of growth, although growth itself seems likely to continue until 2100 and beyond.

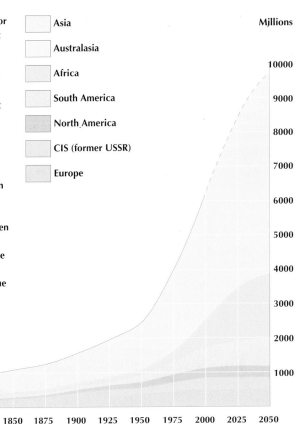

Asia
Australasia
Africa
South America
North America
CIS (former USSR)
Europe

Millions

10000
9000
8000
7000
6000
5000
4000
3000
2000
1000

1750 1775 1800 1825 1850 1875 1900 1925 1950 1975 2000 2025 2050

The Earth's resources

The huge weight of human numbers places enormous demands on the Earth's resources. Our food still comes from plants and animals, which the land and waters must sustain. Some is wild-raised, most notably the huge quantities of fish caught by the world's fishing fleets, but most is now the product of agriculture.

Through the substitution of crops for wild plants, the tilling, fertilizing and watering of soil, and the replacement of wild animals with livestock, agriculture has altered the natural environment more than any other human activity. As food needs have grown, so land has become farmed both more intensively (requiring greater inputs of energy and water and genetically improved varieties), and more extensively, with agriculture extending onto previously unfarmed lands.

The Earth also supplies the raw materials that we use for shelter and material goods. Some materials come from plants, such as the crops used to make textiles and the trees felled for timber. Wood has been used for building since the beginning of recorded history. Much is now the product of tree plantations, but immense quantities are still harvested from wild forests. Other raw materials, minerals, metals and plastics, come directly or indirectly from non-living stores deposited and transformed over millions of years by geological processes and extracted from the Earth.

Nature provides the energy for industry, homes and motor vehicles. Again, some, including fuelwood, is harvested, but a great deal of it is taken from geological reserves of coal, oil and natural gas (which are collectively known as fossil fuels) and uranium ore. We also harness the dynamics of nature, principally by using the energy of falling water to generate hydroelectricity.

Two other resources of the biosphere that are just as indispensable to human survival as they ever were are fresh water and clean air. Air is, of course, easy to come by (although its quality cannot always be assured), but we may have to go to great lengths to secure enough water for our homes, farms and industry.

Global contrasts

World population and resource consumption are greater now than they have ever been. Both are still rising across most of the globe, but the pattern of population growth is far from even and levels of consumption are by no means in keeping with the distribution of people.

Rates of population increase are lowest in those upper-income countries that were among the first to industrialize. Most countries in western Europe, for instance, now have near-stable populations. Birth rates within them have generally fallen in recent decades because of social changes and widespread birth control.

By contrast, birth rates are high across much of Africa, South Asia and Latin America. On average, women in most African countries give birth more than six times during their lives. Lack of health care and education, and of family planning facilities, are among the factors conspiring with tradition to keep fertility high. Populations in lower-income countries are therefore still expanding fast. They already have over 70 per cent of the world's people and, if present trends continue, will contribute the bulk of the projected increase in the world's population during the next century.

Consumption, on the other hand, is by far the highest in industrialized nations, which consume a grossly disproportionate share of energy, minerals, food, water and other resources. Much of what they use comes from lower-income regions of the world through international trade.

Energy consumption is highly uneven (see box below). So is the use of metals from mineral ores. The United States, for example, with less than a quarter of the population of China, consumes twice as much steel, five times as much lead and ten times as much nickel. Disparities in food consumption are less dramatic, but have major implications for nutrition and health. The average citizen of the lower-income countries consumes 2,380 calories per day, compared with 3,380 calories for somebody in an upper-income country.

Energy consumption compared

The consumption of commercial energy (which comes from such sources as fossil fuels, hydro-electricty, and nuclear and geothermal power) differs enormously from country to country. About one quarter of the world's countries consume over three quarters of the world's commercial energy. These countries have only about one quarter of the world's population. On average, someone in one of the highest consumption countries consumes 18 times the commercial energy used by a person in one of the lowest consumption nations. The extremes for total energy consumption, expressed in the equivalent to kilogrammes of coal, range from over 10,000 kilogrammes per person to under 100 kilogrammes.

This also means that the average person in a high consumption country generates more pollution. A North American inhabitant, for example, causes the emission of twice as much carbon dioxide from burning fossil fuel as does a South American, and ten times as much as someone living in South Asia or East Asia (excluding Japan).

By comparing population trends with resource use, a stark truth becomes apparent. The countries with the highest birth rates are the ones with least access to resources. As things stand, most already have great difficulty meeting their needs for food, water, health care, sanitation, housing, jobs, energy and productive land. Rapid population growth only adds to these difficulties and further undermines prospects for sustainable development.

Governments in lower-income countries must draw on scarce financial reserves or add to their foreign debt to meet basic needs. This in turn often prompts them to increase demands on their stocks of timber, fish, petroleum and other resources. But resources and the biosphere itself have their limits.

The countries with the highest birth rates are the ones with least access to resources

Right In Cameroon, a man poses proudly with some of his family of six wives and thirty children. Such high fertility rates are common in many countries of the world, especially in Africa. Both cultural values and economic necessity often encourage large families.

Below Poor living conditions in a mining town in China. Population rises are often highest in towns and cities because of migration from rural areas. The resulting crowded conditions frequently lead to severe problems of pollution and lack of resources.

Carrying capacity

With population and the consumption of resources continuing to increase, carrying capacity has to become an ever more pressing consideration. The concept of carrying capacity is that the number of individuals that can survive in a given area without severely damaging the ecosystem is limited by the amount of food, water, other resources, and ultimately space, that the area can provide.

Application of the concept in a limited area can be easily demonstrated. Ranchers know that they cannot maintain the quality of their range for grazing if they exceed a certain stocking density. The grass supply starts to dwindle, there is too little to go round and the livestock start to go hungry. The carrying capacity of the land has been exceeded.

Logic suggests that the idea could be applied to any species, including humans, on any scale up to the biosphere itself. Thus, there will be finite limits to the human carrying capacity of any ecosystem – limits to the human demands that it can withstand without dangerous deterioration. The limits are a product not only of how many people there are, but also of how much each uses and wastes.

Deleterious impacts on the environment, such as pollution, can diminish an ecosystem's carrying capacity. On the other hand, carrying capacity for people can be stretched by technological advances, although only up to a point and usually with some damage to supporting ecosystems. For example, draining wetlands to increase the extent of arable farmland may lower the water table and cause decreases in many animal and plant species.

While it may be virtually impossible to quantify human carrying capacity for a region or even a locality, especially given social, economic and technological dimensions, we can be sure that limits exist. There are ample cases where the carrying capacity of land has been exceeded or diminished. For example, excessive tree felling for timber, fuelwood and land cultivation has exhausted and degraded soils in many places.

Other resources have come into short supply. Securing an adequate, unpolluted water supply is becoming an increasingly difficult problem for many people who live in arid and semi-arid regions. On an international scale, reserves of lead and nickel have been steadily dwindling – their ores are being exploited faster than the rate at which new reserves are being discovered.

Family size

- 1 child
- 2 children or more
- 3 children or more
- 4 children or more
- 5 children or more
- 6 children or more

The consequences of exceeding carrying capacity are not merely environmental or economic; shortages of vital resources create misery and can lead to social instability and civil strife. Scarcities of renewable resources are already contributing to violent conflicts in many parts of the developing world. If suffering and conflict are not to embroil more nations, we must take steps to keep within or return to within carrying capacities. This is even more important if we remember that we are seeking not just survival, but a sustainable improvement in the quality of life of several billion people.

Within the limits

To stay within the Earth's carrying capacity and well enough clear of its limits for real improvement in human quality of life, it is essential to keep population growth and resource consumption in check. The actions needed will vary greatly from nation to nation – and among communities within nations – because of the wide variations there are in population size, population growth rates, religious beliefs, human needs, resource-consumption patterns and resource availability. By and large, however, the most important tasks are for lower-income countries to reduce birth rates and for higher-income countries to rein in consumption.

To stay within Earth's carrying capacity, we must keep population growth and resource consumption in check

Stabilizing population and putting resource use on a more equitable and sustainable footing are the greatest challenges of our time, and they touch human sensitivity deeply. Cutting consumption can come through gains in efficiency and a stabilization of living standards for those with a good standard of living. It is unrealistic to expect people willingly to reduce that standard, yet all of us need to alter our lifestyles in some ways, for the sake of a decent standard of living for our contemporaries and a dignified future for our descendants.

The UN estimates that population growth will start levelling off everywhere during the next century, ultimately stabilizing at somewhere between 11 and 12 billion people. This assumes that the average number of children born alive to a woman in her lifetime will fall to 3.3 births by the year 2000. If fertility rates do not decline to this level, the population could become even larger, unless environmental degradation leads to a substantial increase in the death rate.

A successful effort to cut birth rates below the projected level would enable the world population to stabilize at 10 billion. The task is enormous but feasible: in the past 20 years, China, Cuba, Singapore and Thailand more than halved their fertility rates. Another 16 countries have cut theirs by between 40 and 50 per cent.

People limit family size when it makes sense to them socially and economically: when men accept changes in the roles of women and no longer see large families as being a source of prestige; when women's education and status in society improve; when families can survive without relying on the income from children (for some, a large family is seen as being a living pension); and when rates of child mortality drop.

Improving standards of education and health has a major impact on fertility. Women who have completed primary school have fewer children than those with no schooling. As the education level of mothers rise, so families become smaller.

Above A health worker monitors infant body-weight at a post-natal clinic in Bangladesh. Improvements in medical care have greatly reduced infant mortality in many parts of the world. While the most obvious effect of these improvements is to increase population, it also has the effect of encouraging women to have fewer children because they can be more certain that those that they do have will survive.

In four Latin American countries education was found to be responsible for 40–60 per cent of the decline in fertility registered over the past decade. Furthermore, better health provision gives each child a better chance of survival – another impetus for women to wait before conceiving again.

In many cases, wise health policy includes promoting breast feeding. The use of milk formula under unhygienic conditions by families who neither need nor can afford it kills babies and increases fertility. Breast feeding is also an effective traditional method of child-spacing. More births are averted in sub-Saharan Africa by ovulation suppression during breast feeding than by the use of modern methods of contraception.

Family planning

In 1990, some 381 million couples in the lower-income countries used a family-planning method. To achieve the UN population projection of 6.4 billion by the year 2000, an additional 186 million couples must be using contraception by the end of the century. Despite traditional opposition, family-planning is widely desired. Surveys conducted in a large number of lower-income countries show that 50-80 per cent of married women wish to space or limit their childbearing.

This need is not being met, however. In Africa, less than a quarter of women not wanting any more births are practising contraception; in Asia the figure is 43 per cent, and in Latin America it is 57 per cent. Perhaps a quarter of all pregnancies in lower-income countries end in abortion, often because contraception is not available. It has been estimated that family planning alone would save the lives of 200,000 women and five million children by helping couples to space their children and avoid high-risk pregnancies.

Family planning is underfunded. Many services cannot expand because their supply of contraceptives is not assured. Some actually run out. Currently, $4.5 billion per year is spent on family planning services in the lower-income countries.

Improving standards of education and health reduces fertility rates

Of this sum, only $700 million comes from higher-income countries – just 1.3 per cent of their development assistance. For a successful programme, the total spent each year needs to be increased to $9 billion per year by 2000, with $4.5 billion coming from development assistance. These are not impossible sums. The money saved by lower expenditure on maternal and child health could be greater than the initial costs of family planning.

Wherever realistic family-planning facilities have been made available, fertility has declined. Experience from 83 countries shows that a 15 per cent increase in contraceptive availability decreases fertility by nearly one child per woman. With effective programmes, birth rates have fallen two to seven times faster in lower-income countries than they did in Europe and North America during a similar transition from high to low fertility.

Below Village children being taught to read and write in Shahdara near Islamabad, Pakistan. Learning to read and write will not only improve these children's opportunities to lead fulfilling lives, but also increase their abilities to contribute to society. It has been clearly shown that improved education, especially for women, leads to reduced family sizes. This fact alone is a compelling argument for greater access to education for all people.

Reducing consumption

Every nation should make progress towards resource conservation, ensuring that people's use of all resources is managed for sustainability. But the upper-income countries have a special responsibility. They and their citizens must make a concerted effort to reduce their huge consumption of energy and raw materials. Between 1970 and 1986, several countries lowered their per capita energy consumption through greater efficiency: for example, the United States (down by 12 per cent), Luxembourg (by 33 per cent), United Kingdom (by 10 per cent) and Denmark (by 15 per cent). But most of the other big consumers increased it.

For resources to be conserved while quality of life is improved, three main kinds of action must be taken, preferably at the same time. First, new and more efficient technologies must be developed.

Second, national economic and regulatory policies must vigorously promote the switch to a less wasteful (and therefore less polluting) society. Third, individuals must understand how they can gain from changes in their own activities and consumption patterns, and begin to demand products with lower environmental impacts.

The development of technologies that produce and use energy and materials more efficiently, including recycling, makes long-term economic sense for industry. Government economic incentives can make it easier in the short term, with regulations and standards also forcing the pace of change. In the United Kingdom, a Better Environmental Awards for Industry scheme has operated for some years, as a partnership between government, industry and a national non-governmental organization (NGO) that runs the scheme.

Above Tropical timber planks made from trees that have been replaced by the logging company. Although replanting is a long-term investment, it is the only way that the timber industry can become a sustainable activity. Indeed, support for properly managed logging and reforestation programmes can help to conserve forests. For example, the land is safeguarded against incursions of agricultural settlers who would destroy the forest and whose crops and animals would take the fertility from the soil and prevent eventual regrowth.

Below Preparing metal containers for re-use in Colombo, Sri Lanka. In lower-income countries, recycling is long-established as an "industry", encouraged by economic necessity at a local level, and is usually carried out by individual entrepreneurs. In the higher-income countries there is less motivation to undertake recycling.

Above Cooking on a fuelwood stove in Zimbabwe. In many lower-income regions, people rely on wood for cooking and other energy needs; the demand often exceeds what can be taken sustainably – despite much lower overall energy consumption than in higher-income countries. Replanting of fuelwood and, even more importantly, finding alternative energy sources and making them widely available are essential.

Taxes and consumers

Taxing use of energy and other resources is one method of inducing efficient technology and consumption patterns both in industry and in the home. Each government needs to work out within the circumstances of its own country how this can be brought about without increasing poverty. It is not difficult to do this while keeping the overall tax burden on an enconomy unchanged – income tax, for example, can be lowered to offset price rises. Electricity and fuel credits could be given to pensioners and others on low incomes.

This approach would get round the present political objection that resource taxes are additional to existing taxes so are politically unacceptable. Here it is proposed that resource taxes wholly or partially replace existing taxes. Such taxes are consistent with the User Pays Principle, which argues that prices in all parts of an economy should reflect the full social cost of the use or depletion of a resource.

Consumers have a strong contribution to make through their buying power. As "green" consumers, each of us can do something positive, however serious the problem, and whatever the government of the day is doing. Consumers can switch from one brand to another, perhaps one that uses recycled materials, or stop buying a product if it represents the unnecessary use of a scarce resource or one harvested and processed by unsustainable means. The cumulative effect of "green" actions by millions of people can significantly change patterns of resource consumption.

Technologies that recycle non-renewable materials, and use less of these resources for a particular product or switch to renewable substitutes are particularly important if we are to extend the life of the reserves that remain.

It is important that governments and aid agencies in high-income countries support the transfer of efficient technologies to lower-income countries through both capital aid and technical assistance. Present energy-wasting practices, in such areas as energy production and transmission, and in industry, impose an unnecessary burden on the countries concerned; where this is the case, speedy replacement of technology should be a key objective. Another objective would be to provide and promote more efficient domestic stoves to replace the presently widespread but wasteful wood-burning stoves. The scope for gain in these sectors is very large. If China were to achieve the energy efficiency of an average high-income country, it would be able to double its economic output without building any more power stations.

Consumers can significantly change patterns of resource consumption

If they are to do this, however, consumers need reliable information. At present, lack of standards and reliable labelling hampers informed choice.

Decisions about environmental acceptability will always be matters of judgement. We often do not know all the environmental effects of products and there are difficult choices. For example, is cotton better than polyester because synthetic fibres use up non-renewable resources? Or is polyester better because cotton growers use a lot of pesticides and fertilizers? Despite such problems, the government of Germany has set up a national scheme to identify and promote "environment-friendly" products, and this is now being broadened to cover the whole European Community.

Priority Actions

1

Increase awareness of the need to stabilize population and resource consumption

Through discussion, education and publicity, individuals, schools, NGOs, businesses and governments should spread the word that:
• The carrying capacity of the Earth is not something unlimited
• Population stabilization is essential, and men and women must accept their shared responsibility for achieving it
• Excessive and wasteful use of resources brings us closer to the limits of the carrying capacity of the Earth
• People in upper-income countries can eliminate wasteful consumption without reducing their quality of life, and often with financial savings.

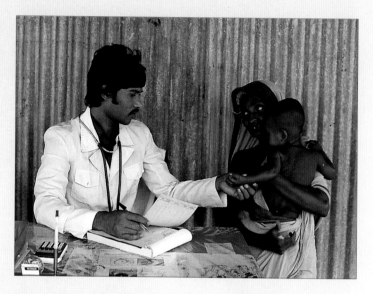

2

Integrate population and resource consumption issues in national policies and planning

Explicit government policies to limit population and consumption are needed, and they should play a key role in national development planning. The policies and plans should:
• Set goals for stabilizing population at a sustainable level
• Set goals for reducing the consumption of energy and other resources to a sustainable level in the high-consumption countries of the world
• Set goals for higher, but sustainable, agricultural production in low-consumption countries
• Encourage the private sector and NGOs to carry out programmes that support family planning and reduced consumption of resources.

3

Fund family planning services in lower-income countries

The support for family planning by governments and international aid agencies must increase to meet both existing demands and the need further to reduce fertility rates. For programmes to succeed, this means:
• Doubling annual expenditure on family planning, with half the total to come from overseas aid
• Ensuring that family planning is an integral part of all rural and urban development programmes and is funded as part of their budgets
• Advising people on the full range of alternative methods available (traditional or natural, barrier, hormonal or surgical) and helping them to make choices appropriate to their wants and needs.

4

Improve maternal and child health care

Better health provision can go a long way to reducing the frequency of births. Dramatic results can come from inexpensive health services that provide:
• Family planning services
• Antenatal and postnatal care at the local level, especially giving food supplements to undernourished pregnant and lactating women, and encouraging breast feeding
• Education for women, men and children on the importance of simple hygiene, such as sanitary treatment of food and drinking water, and safe disposal of human waste.

5
Develop, test and adopt resource-efficient technologies

Using both non-renewable and renewable resources more efficiently can save money and stimulate technological innovation, as well as reduce consumption and pollution. To foster the adoption of suitable new technologies, high-income countries should:
• Make use of economic incentives and regulations to encourage industries and public utilities to adopt and invest in resource-efficient technology
• Establish awards for environmentally sound processes and products
• Make improved technology and technical assistance readily available to lower-income countries.

6
Tax energy and other resources in high-consumption countries

Replacing some existing taxes with taxes on the use of energy and other resources can encourage more efficient technology, less waste and pollution, greater use of renewable rather than non-renewable resources, and more durable products. Governments in high-consumption countries should:
• First remove any subsidies and other factors that distort prices, except the subsidies that have been introduced to promote sustainability
• If necessary, introduce taxes so that the prices of resources match their real cost to society as closely as possible. Governments in other countries, while seeking the same goal, should:
• Introduce such measures more gradually and specifically, applying them first to sectors where consumption is particularly high and wasteful.

7
Become a "green" consumer

Domestic consumption of resources can be made more efficient with simple actions such as improving insulation and sorting waste for recycling. Consumers, especially those in upper-income countries, can also use their buying power to strengthen the market for goods that do the least possible harm to the environment. They can do so by:
• Becoming informed consumers of products and services
• Asking for environmentally friendly products at retailers
• Telling manufacturers and retailers the reasons for choosing certain products or brands and avoiding others
• Informing others about the issues: writing to local and national media, to utilities and to legislators
• Encouraging family, friends, neighbours and co-workers to do the same.

Far left Participants in a National Wildlife Seminar in Niger, study an educational wall chart. Increasing people's awareness of issues of conservation and sustainability is essential and will require spreading information about such matters as the effects of the unsustainable use of resources and the limits to the carrying capacities of particular regions or of the Earth as a whole.

Above left A medical aid worker examines a child with its mother in Bangladesh as part of a healthcare project funded by a European aid organization. As well as dealing with the problems of disease, it is essential that family planning is an increasing part of such services provided by aid organizations and governments, involving both advice and supplying the means of contraception.

Above Coolant gas (which contains ozone-destroying CFCS) is safely removed from an old refrigerator at a public recycling centre in Paris, France. Without the gas, it will be possible to recycle safely other materials in the refrigerator. Taking the time and trouble (and spending money when necessary) to conserve resources and avoid pollution is a personal as well as a public responsibility.

The Development Imperative

Development means increasing society's ability to meet human needs. Economic growth may be an important component of development, but it cannot be a goal in itself. The real aim must be to improve the quality of human existence – to enable people to enjoy long, healthy and fulfilling lives. At present, for huge numbers of people, life is hard, insecure and unfulfilling.

The major requirements for a satisfactory life fall into two categories. In the first are those that meet people's basic physical needs, namely adequate food, safe drinking water, shelter, sanitation and health care. In the second are those that enable people fully to develop their own potential and contribute to society. Such requirements include education, employment opportunities, access to the resources needed for a decent standard of living, peace, political freedom and freedom from prejudice based on race, religion or sex.

Although the world has come closer to meeting human requirements during the past 30 years, significant shortfalls remain in both categories. The shortfalls are greatest in the lower-income countries of the world (across much of Asia, Africa, Latin America and the Caribbean), but persistent inequality in upper-income countries means that large sections of their populations are also denied a dignified quality of life.

While providing basic needs for all the world's people is clearly of the greatest urgency, the two categories of human development are interrelated and it is difficult to meet the requirements of either one without paying adequate attention to the other. Development is only real if it makes our lives better in all respects.

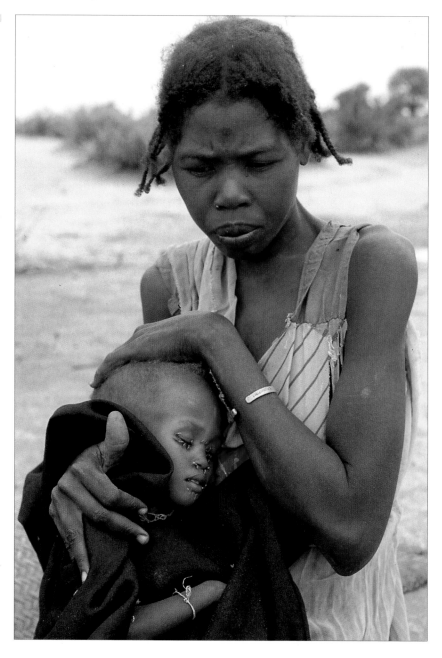

Global shortfalls

The majority of people today, mostly but not all living in lower-income countries, have standards of living ranging from the miserable to the barely tolerable. They use far less than their arithmetical share of Earth's resources and in many cases suffer from the diseases of poverty (linked to malnutrition and compounded by inadequate health care).

Comparing average incomes per head among the nations of the world, it has been estimated that the wealthiest 20 per cent of global population receives nearly 83 per cent of total world income. By stark contrast, the poorest 20 per cent gets less than 1.5 per cent. Because these figures conceal disparities within nations, the true share of income received by the very poorest sectors of society around the world is even more pitiful.

Absolute poverty implies an income inadequate to meet basic physical needs. No fewer than one billion people live at or below the absolute poverty level; by the end of the century the figure is likely to be 1.3 billion. The biggest increase is expected in Africa – from about 270 million to 400 million.

Hunger is felt on a massive scale. About 100 million people were affected by famine in 1990, and more than a quarter of all people do not get enough food for adequate health. Ethiopians get only two-thirds of the food energy they need.

In addition, lack of income, materials and land rights forces millions around the world to live in cramped, dangerous dwellings, vulnerable to rainstorms, high winds, floods and landslides, with little or no access to clean water or power. Around 2.3 billion people do not have proper sanitation.

Above **A mother and her child in Sudan, refugees from war and famine. There is a vast amount of hunger in the world, not only in regions affected by famine, and all too often the problems are made worse by political, religious and ethnic conflicts that stand in the way of human development.**

Readily preventable diseases still take millions of lives every year. Children are particularly vulnerable. In the poorest nations, the infant mortality rate is 115 per 1,000 live births, compared to only 13 per 1,000 in the industrialized countries.

Illiteracy and unemployment lock the poor more tightly into poverty. About 950 million adults in lower-income countries can neither read nor write; nearly two thirds of them are women. In Nepal, only one in four adults is literate. Shortage of paid jobs in developing countries forces many children and families to make a living hawking wares and services on city streets.

Gains and losses

Despite the enormous shortfalls, lower-income countries have achieved major successes in recent decades. Average life expectancy has risen from 46 to 63 years (but it is still below 50 years in 19 countries). Access to safe water has increased in the past 20 years by two thirds. Now some 80 per cent of the urban population of lower-income countries has supplies of drinking water.

Child mortality rates halved between 1960 and 1990, and adult literacy has increased by more than one third since 1970. By the late 1980s, over 70 per cent of children were completing primary education. Calorie supplies increased as food production per head kept pace with or outstripped population growth in Asia and Latin America. On all these measures the disparities between lower and upper-income countries are steadily shrinking.

However, there are worrying trends. Global food production has increased, but surpluses have tended to be where they are not needed, with starvation elsewhere. Food production in Africa fell by 8 per cent between 1978 and 1988.

Measures of higher education – important for economic progress – show a widening gap between rich and poor. In developing countries, university graduates make up 1.2 per cent of their age group; in industrial countries they make up 9.4 per cent.

> ### Development is only real if it makes everyone's lives better in all respects.

Income gaps have also widened. The income disparity noted above between the richest and poorest in the world has doubled since 1960; and growth in national income does not automatically reach all citizens. For instance, Brazil ranks above most developing countries in income per capita, but the top 20 per cent of its citizens earn 26 times as much as the bottom 20 per cent.

Below An elderly couple make slow and painful progress toward a food centre in Somalia organized by the International Committee of the Red Cross. In many lower-income countries of the world, the chances of a child living to such old age are relatively small: in Somalia – as in 18 other countries – life expectancy is less than 50 years, even without the ravages of war or famine.

Illiteracy

Under 10%

10-25%

25-50%

50-75%

Over 75%

Above The map shows for each country the percentage of the population unable to read or write (figures from the latest available year). The general trend is for the higher rates of illiteracy to be in lower-income countries, but this is by no means always the case. Such influences as social attitudes (particularly towards the education of women) and government policy can have a large effect on literacy rates. For example, Guyana has an illiteracy rate of only 4 per cent. (Separate statistics for the republics of the former Soviet Union and Yugoslavia are not available.)

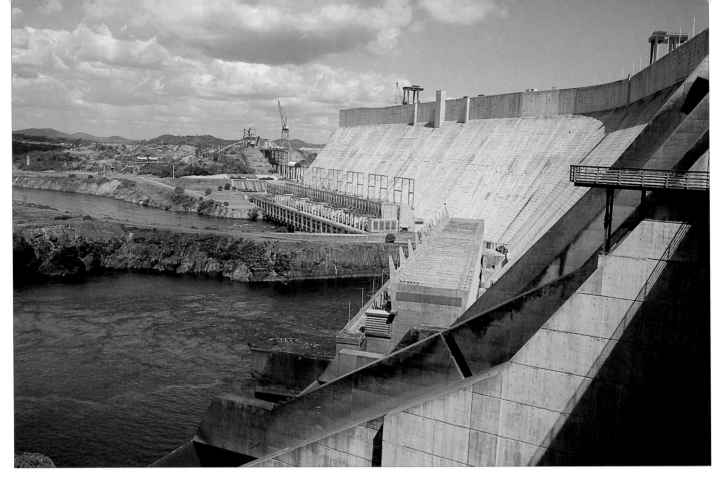

Arrested development

Many factors combine to retard investment in social and environmental programmes and limit the progress in human development. Some of them could be dealt with by the countries themselves, including problems of corruption, inefficiency, failure to institute a fair taxation system and deliberate choice to invest in other sectors.

Development investments in some countries have concentrated on facilitating the exploitation of resources and building up processing plants, factories, infrastructure and armaments, while providing far too little support for health, education, and welfare services or measures that would conserve resources and safeguard the environment. Countries such as Iraq and Somalia are good examples of countries that have this imbalance in the allocation of investments.

Other causes that limit the progress of human development, such as lack of export earnings, high interest payments on loans and insufficient development assistance, can only be dealt with by changes in global economic relationships. The effects of the international economic situation weigh heavily on poor nations and most heavily on their poorest citizens.

The purchasing power of lower-income countries has declined in recent decades, as a result of both the way world markets work and the burden of debt. Lower-income countries gain much of their revenue by exporting commodities such as minerals, timber and cash crops. But the prices of many of these on the world market have fallen by

a third or more since 1970. At the same time, the cost of borrowing for development projects from overseas governments and banks has risen sharply, leaving many countries struggling to meet even the interest payments on the loans. Since 1970, the indebtedness of the developing world has soared from around $200 billion to over $1,000 billion.

The poorest and most debt-ridden countries have the greatest difficulty in securing resources for human development – and the greatest need. Many of them have above-average rates of human population growth, yet government revenues and average incomes are declining. In many, living conditions are becoming intolerable. As a result of human desperation, pressures on natural resources are increasing, and too many countries are suffering a vicious spiral of degradation which will further undermine their long-term prospects.

Poverty within wealth

The United Nations Development Programme has devised a method of comparing the levels of development found in different countries. Its Human Development Index combines statistics on national income, life expectancy and educational attainment to try to give a measure of progress in each country relative to others. Not surprisingly, the countries that score highest on the index include Canada, Japan, Australia, New Zealand, the United States and most of those in Europe. While such countries have achieved high living standards, levels of health care and standards of education, disparities and shortfalls remain.

In Australia, New Zealand, the United States and Switzerland, the personal income of the highest 20 per cent during the 1980s was more than 8.5 times that of the lowest 20 per cent of people. In virtually all upper-income countries a segment of the population is poorly housed, malnourished and lacks the capacity to improve its position.

The problem of unemployment is serious and widespread, wasting human resources, provoking social unrest and preventing personal fulfilment. The homeless have to endure the cold of winter outdoors, and many of the poor cannot afford to heat their dwellings properly. Discrimination on the grounds of sex and race is widespread in many countries. In Japan, average female wages are 50 per cent those of men. Many ethnic minorities in upper-income countries usually suffer low income levels and high unemployment.

Affluence has not protected high-income countries or the wealthy minority in poor countries from social problems – from such things as drug and alcohol abuse, family breakdown and violence. Clearly, such models of development are not an ideal for others to pursue.

Affluence has not protected high-income countries from social problems

Above Brazil nuts being loaded at the port of Belem on the Amazon River. Cash crops can provide revenue to help fund development. However, that revenue is subject to the fluctuations of world commodity markets, where prices have generally been falling since the 1970s.

Right Homeless people sleeping on the street in London, capital of the United Kingdom and one of the richest cities in the world. Virtually all higher-income countries have problems arising from economic difficulties and social organization and priorities.

Left The Royal Thai Army puts on a seemingly endless display of high-cost military hardware. Many lower- and higher-income countries divert a large proportion of their national revenue to maintaining a well-equipped standing army. Other more productive objects of expenditure are deemed secondary to perceived military imperatives.

Closing the Gap

Development must continue – for the disadvantaged of the world it is an imperative. Humanity must find the means to close the gap not only between rich and poor countries but also between the rich and the poor in all countries. Poverty is not only unjust, it prevents people and societies from living sustainably. Meanwhile, modern media and tourism bring the luxury of the rich before the eyes of the poor, who no longer patiently accept disparity as part of some inevitable order. A global society characterized by inequity cannot endure.

As is stressed in other chapters, sustainable global development requires a freeing of economic resources and opportunity for those countries most in need. Cancellation of foreign debt and improvements in conditions of trade offer ways forward. Greater international financial assistance is needed for social purposes and to support the conservation and rehabilitation of natural resources. Aid for social purposes is more important than that for major capital development.

Development success in Sri Lanka and Costa Rica

Some countries with relatively low incomes have good records in human development. Priority in these countries is given to programmes that help to maintain health, build the capacities of individual citizens and provide a safety net for those faced with adverse economic change.

As early as 1945, Sri Lanka extended free medical care to almost every part of the country and introduced universal free education up to university level. The country also has a long-standing history of food subsidies. Despite a per capita income one tenth of that in the United States, daily calorie supplies are 106 per cent of requirements, the literacy rate is 88 per cent, and 93 per cent of the people have access to health services.

In a similar way, Costa Rica, which has a per capita income that is just over one fifth of the United States average, has managed to achieve human development indicators close to those of Europe. Without an army, it is one of the few countries that incurs no military expenditure. Costa Rica has given a high priority to education and was a pioneer in providing basic health services, emphasizing preventive measures, to the whole population. All but a few per cent of the population have access to adequate sanitation. The citizens of Costa Rica enjoy a daily calorie intake almost 25 per cent above the minimum requirement, a literacy rate of 93 per cent and a life expectancy comparable with that of Germany.

All governments of the world need to review their budgetary priorities to release finance for lasting development and aid. Military expenditures worldwide, which in 1989 totalled some $826 billion, create no lasting benefits and are widely regarded as an obvious source of savings for redeployment. Following up international agreements on arms limitations, military expenditures should be reduced to the minimum needed for security. Some personnel, vehicles and equipment could be redeployed for conservation and development projects and used for disaster relief.

Poverty is not only unjust, it prevents people and societies from living sustainably

Domestic policies to sustain or restore national economies are critical for all lower-income countries. The policies needed will vary according to national environmental, cultural and political circumstances. In many cases, there is scope for a liberalization of national markets. Economic performance is likely to improve if market systems are enabled to work efficiently, but regulatory measures need to be taken to prevent damage to the environment and to cushion the social impact of sudden change.

Social policies

An increase in gross national product (GNP) – the economic value of a country's annual output of goods and services – is widely regarded as the main goal of development. It provides the essential means to meet basic needs and improve living conditions, but, as the poor in upper-income countries know only too well, it does not guarantee quality of life for all citizens and should not be the main focus of development.

Many fast-growing lower-income countries are already discovering that high GNP growth does not automatically reduce social and economic deprivation. For that to happen, more positively directed social policies are needed. By contrast, some lower-income countries such as Costa Rica and Sri Lanka have shown that relatively poor nations can reach high levels of human development if they skilfully use the human abilities and resources available to them (see box opposite).

Good social policies can redistribute resources, and thereby compensate to some degree for poor income distribution. Targeted income support for the poorest can be one way of ensuring that economic development helps those who need it most.

Left A closed and abandoned coal mine in northern Britain. The decline of the coal industry in Britain has caused considerable hardship arising from unemployment. High GNPs in the higher-income countries have not prevented many economic and social problems. Although most such countries have some support for the unemployed through direct cash payments, retraining has become an urgent social priority.

Far left A tourist photographs a man displaying a snake in Patan, Nepal. Tourism is a valuable source of income for many countries. However, the obvious wealth of many tourists, combined with the global perspective provided by modern media, bring the disparities in income between different parts of the world to the attention of some of the world's poorer citizens.

Left At a village school in Sri Lanka, young children acquire the literacy that will form the foundation for their future education. Thanks to a policy of free education for all, Sri Lanka now has a skilful and adaptable workforce in a good position to take advantage of any new economic opportunities, as and when they arise.

Direct cash payments can help households in extreme poverty and such payments are common in richer countries. They are less suited for lower-income countries where many more families are in need and the administrative machinery is weaker, although Chile is one example of a country that has made use of them.

Food subsidies, if the are properly targeted at low-income households and managed so as not to reduce the incentive for people to produce food, can do much to ensure that food is affordable for everybody. In the early 1970s, such food subsidies increased consumption by the poorest 15 per cent of urban Bangladesh by 15–25 per cent. In many poor societies, they can provide a social safety net at reasonable cost (1–2 per cent of GNP). In high-income countries, food subsidies have often compensated for inadequate social security schemes. Special nutrition programmes can also be designed for particular groups. For example, Chile and Botswana have used free school lunch schemes in primary schools to combat extreme malnutrition in children (such schemes also encourage attendance and improve pupils' concentration).

Improvements for all

Targeted schemes to combat the worst poverty should be combined with improvements in basic health care and education for everyone in the community. Many lower-income countries, however, put only half as much of their budgets into health and education in 1990 as in the 1970s. Primary health care provision is relatively cheap and effective and needs to be applied on a wider scale.

Improving the status of women in all countries is crucial

Care can involve community-based diagnosis and treatment of common illnesses, midwifery services, immunization, and advice and help with hygiene. Simple remedies (such as oral rehydration with a mixture of sugars and salts in water in cases of acute diarrhoea) could save many lives, but often expensive and less effective drugs are promoted.

More progress is needed in providing primary schooling for those children who at present receive no education and to end the current high drop-out rates in primary schools, which sometimes climb above 70 per cent. Providing universal primary schooling would require annual increases in expenditure well over double the rates of previous years. But investment in sending children to school and ensuring their attendance has a high pay-off because it equips them to make a greater economic contribution to society. More international assistance should be made available for both health and education programmes.

Improving the status of women in all countries is crucial (see box opposite). Poverty and stressful living conditions tend to bear most heavily on women, especially as women are likely to have the principal responsibility for running households and caring for children. All too frequently, female education is hampered by biases deeply rooted in tradition. Girls are the most likely to be withdrawn from school for social reasons, and female literacy consistently lags behind male literacy. Further biases exist in the workplace.

Key progress includes giving women access to the means of controlling their own fertility and the size of their families. Reforms should be instituted that give women a full voice in political, bureaucratic and economic decisions at all levels.

Above A women sells her goods at a market on Nosy-Be Island, Madagascar. Although women perform key economic roles in all societies, they often have limited access to training and credit and little control over income. This situation should be changed, not least so that the potential contribution of women to the development of society will be fully realized.

Below On the streets of Jakarta, Indonesia, children try to hawk newspapers and cigarettes to passing motorists. This is not motivated by a desire for "pocket money", but by economic necessity. Those fortunate enough to have families may be the primary breadwinners. Others may be entirely alone, fending for themselves. Elsewhere in the city, thousands of other children work in workshops, factories and restaurants, often in dangerous and unhealthy conditions. In places where adult labour is cheap, child labour is even cheaper. Child exploitation is widespread, but without the additional income many families would go hungry.

Bottom Backstreet life in Ethiopia. Women and children often bear the brunt of slum conditions. Living in such an environment, where poverty, lack of resources and miserable surrounding are oppressive, it is hard for people to see beyond the immediate future, let alone nurture hopes and aspirations for improving their situations.

Women's role in the community

In most countries, women have limited access to, and control over, income, credit, land, education, training, health care and information. They also tend to suffer the worst effects of poverty and environmental degradation. As a result, many lack the opportunity for self-fulfilment, and potential contributions to the community are lost. Crucial steps that can be taken to help women improve their status include:

• Providing universal suffrage
• Upholding legislation to ensure equal pay for equal work, equal representation of women in on-the-job training programmes and similar schemes, maternity leave benefits, and provisions for day care of dependants
• Increasing economic opportunities for women by helping them set up businesses, providing training in business management and fostering savings and loans facilities for women
• Providing education for women, giving priority to extending mandatory primary schooling for women – especially in rural areas – and ensuring equal representation in secondary schooling and vocational training
• Reviewing laws that have an impact on family size, such as raising the minimum legal age for marriage to 18 years
• Providing access to family planning and ensuring that health and nutrition programmes cater for the needs of mothers, especially during pregnancy and following birth.

Priorities for progress

Clearly, strategies for improving the quality of life will vary from country to country. For most lower-income countries, improving the economy will remain a high priority for some time. They will need both to increase incomes and to devote a greater proportion of their budgets to social spending and environmental protection.

Upper-income countries tend to have a different agenda, since virtually all of them have already achieved high average levels of human development (exceptions are the United Arab Emirates, Saudi Arabia, Oman, Libya and South Africa). The principal challenges to upper-income countries are to reduce inequality and discrimination among their populations and to enhance the quality of life of all citizens, while reducing energy and resource consumption and curbing pollution. They face a difficult but achievable task in making those changes and at the same time maintaining employment and industrial activity.

Priority Actions

1

In lower-income countries, increase economic growth to advance human development

In lower-income countries the challenge is to achieve faster and longer-term economic growth to secure satisfactory living standards and to finance investment in human development and environmental conservation. The policies and assistance that are required include:
- Opening international markets to ensure that poorer countries can sell their produce at prices that give a reasonable rate of return
- Measures to attract foreign investment and technology
- Investment in future skills. As an aid to sustainable development, 15–20 per cent of national income should go into investment, with special emphasis on science, technology, education, training and health provision
- Fair access to land and resources in order to enable all people to improve their incomes, living standards and economic productivity.

- More resources to rural areas to reduce rural-urban disparities
- Provision of greater employment opportunities to raise incomes and spread the benefits throughout the population. Industrialization is urgently needed, but it must be carried out in ways that safeguard the environment. It must offer:
- Promotion of private initiative, for example, through lending schemes for small and medium-sized enterprises
- Action to help people undertake their own development, for example, increasing their management of local resources and their participation in development decisions, providing vocational training and granting credit
- Social measures to ensure that economic development helps those most in need
- Action to reduce disparities between the genders, and to ensure that women are enabled to play a full part in the process of national development.

Far right Women in Niger, West Africa, draw water from a desert well. Providing people with access to safe and reliable sources of water for drinking and other purposes should be a major benefit and goal of economic development programmes, together with other measures to improve health.

Above Cleaning solar plate collectors in Mauritania. These plates warm water by means of heat from the Sun. Many low-income countries are in regions of the world with relatively high levels of sunlight and so can take advantage of solar plates, which are an easily installed and maintained method of producing hot water at low cost. Solar plates also have virtually no environmental impact, other than occupying an area of land.

Right A stretch of oak woodland in northern England under careful management to produce timber and to preserve the value of the landscape. Conservation and sustainable use are combined with attractive results.

2
In upper-income countries, adjust development policies to ensure sustainability

These countries face just as severe a challenge, but of a different kind. They need to find ways of enhancing everyone's quality of life, while reducing environmental impact. Using regulation and economic measures as appropriate, governments should give high priority to:
• Improvements in the living standards of the poorest inhabitants
• Reduction of consumption, waste and pollution at all levels
• Conservation of landscape, cultural heritage and biological diversity
• New approaches to international economic, trading and political relationships that will help the development of lower-income countries.

3
Provide the services that will promote a long and healthy life

A benefit of economic development should be improved health care. The following targets should be pursued:
• Complete immunization of all children – if lower-income countries maintain past progress, most could immunize all children in less than a decade
• Reducing under-five mortality – female literacy, cleaner water, better sanitation, health care and broader immunization are all linked to higher child survival, and in turn to population stabilization
• Eliminating severe malnutrition – this is within the reach of properly-targeted nutrition programmes, which usually cost little and have a large payoff
• Providing universal access to safe water – most lower-income countries can reach this target if they maintain past progress.

4
Provide education for all

Education that fits people for living sustainably is essential in both upper- and lower-income countries. Basic targets should include:
• Universal primary schooling for all children, which is the most important human development target because it can unleash the potential of so many people
• Ensuring that enrolment leads to attendance; often the key to keeping children in school is investment in high quality and relevant teaching
• Minimized adult illiteracy, and bringing female and male literacy to the same level; citizens' groups and governments can collaborate on literacy programmes.

5
Develop more meaningful indicators of quality of life and monitor achievements

National and international statistics record some of the parameters of quality of life – for example, life expectancy, disease incidence, food availability, education, levels of pollution. There is, however, no established overall quality of life index that can be used for such things as international comparisons and defining goals. Governments, international organizations and the academic community should:
• Review the parameters that might be combined to measure the quality of life
• Support the improvement of the Human Development Index prepared by the UN Development Programme
• Improve systems of social statistics (coverage, reliability, breakdown of data by sex, income group and area)
• Undertake surveys to determine where and how far policies are succeeding in enhancing quality of life, and what the obstacles are to better performance.

The Conservation Imperative

Development is essential, but it will only succeed if it maintains the productivity, resilience and variety of the biosphere. On the other hand, conservation will provide lasting benefits only when it is integrated with the right kinds of development. Just as human societies and economies are interdependent, so their welfare is bound up with that of nature. It is essential, therefore, that development is conservation-based as well as people-centred

Conservation, as outlined in Chapter 3, has three principal aims: to conserve the life-support systems that nature provides; to conserve the diversity of life on Earth; and to ensure that all uses of renewable resources are sustainable.

Life-support systems

The natural processes that take place within the biosphere are essential for sustaining life on our planet. They have helped to shape conditions on Earth to make it possible for life to thrive in its present diversity. At the same time, all organisms, including humans, have evolved in keeping with the prevailing conditions. We are adapted to survive in them and depend on the balance being maintained.

The fine balance of gases in the atmosphere keeps temperatures on the Earth's surface within a tolerable range and filters out potentially lethal ultra-violet radiation. Ecological processes, principally the photosynthesis and respiration of plants, help ensure we have sufficient oxygen to breathe.

Likewise, all of us need a daily supply of fresh water, free from all but a trace of various compounds and microbes that we would consider dangerous contaminants. The cycling of water through vegetation, soil and aquatic organisms helps to

Left Winnowing the rice harvest. Although this scene appears idyllic, like all forms of agriculture there are some associated problems. One is that it almost always involves considerable modification of natural ecosystems, although this may have happened hundreds of years ago.

Far left Like feathered jewels, red-and-green macaws gather at a riverbank clay lick in the Manu Biosphere Reserve, Peru. Macaws are just a tiny part of the enormous and only partly discovered biodiversity of rainforests, perhaps the most productive environment on Earth.

Below A medical research team at Yaounde University, Cameroon, evaluates wild plants for potentially useful substances for medicines. Similar research has made a large number of important discoveries, including drugs that are effective against certain forms of cancer.

The recycling of nutrients by decomposer organisms, as well as the above processes, ensures that we can keep growing the plant and animal food we need. Other ecological processes regenerate the soil and give us the chance to keep harvesting and propagating such useful materials as wood.

These and other ecological processes make up the Earth's life-support systems. Although, to a very limited extent, technology can provide artificial substitutes for ecological processes – such as chemical fertilizers in place of nutrient recycling – it cannot replace life-support systems in full. Moreover, such substitution is economically and environmentally costly. Life-support systems freely and sustainably maintain productivity and capacity for renewal. Because many are living processes, they can respond to environmental change, giving ecosystems a degree of adaptability that prevents changes turning into catastrophes.

Some changes, however, are just too great. Anything that seriously impairs or disrupts life-support systems threatens the stability of ecosystems and the survival of all that depend on them.

In human terms, the most important ecological processes take place in agricultural, forest, coastal and fresh water ecosystems. All are susceptible to environmental damage. Pollution of many kinds destroys soil organisms, attacks vegetation, contaminates water and kills aquatic life. Some soils have been so badly contaminated that they have become entirely unusable.

The clearance of forests, especially in steep-sided river valleys, has often speeded run-off after rainfall, making fresh water supplies irregular downstream. Excessive sewage outflow in some coastal waters disrupts recycling by flooding the system with too many nutrients, creating conditions favourable to the proliferation of poisonous micro-organisms – the so-called "red tides". In these and many other ways that will become apparent in the following chapters, life-support systems are being disrupted on an increasing scale.

Biodiversity

Biological diversity (or "biodiversity") should be conserved as a matter of principle, because all species deserve respect regardless of their use to humanity and because they are all components of one life-support system. However, biodiversity is also of enormous value to us in more direct ways. It provides us with many economic benefits and adds greatly to the quality of our lives.

The diversity of nature is a source of beauty, enjoyment, understanding and knowledge. It is the source of all biological wealth – supplying all of our food and much of our raw materials.

Wild organisms constitute an enormous pool of irreplaceable genetic material and are a source of potential future products of immense value to agriculture, medicine and industry.

Biological diversity is continually changing as evolution gives rise to new species, while new ecological conditions cause others to disappear. By and large, the process is a slow one, and, for any species, takes place over very many generations. Human alteration of the biosphere, by contrast, is now changing ecological conditions at what is often a rapid rate, hastening the depletion and extinction of species.

Threats to species, including destruction or disruption of habitat, toxic pollution, excessive hunting, capture and harvesting and the introduction of non-native species, have been mounting ever since human numbers and demands on resources began to rise. During this century, at least 70 species of bird and more than 50 mammals are known to have become extinct. Many more species have lost part of their genetic variation because they have died out across sections of their range. Because our

knowledge of biodiversity, especially of the myriad tropical plants and insects, is far from complete, the full roll call of all threatened species around the world can only be guessed at, but the number certainly runs into tens of thousands.

With wild habitats long diminished in the industrialized countries, the conversion of natural ecosystems has been gathering pace in developing countries in recent decades. By the mid-1980s, tropical Africa had already lost 65 per cent of its original habitat, and tropical south and east Asia 68 per cent. The most threatened ecosystems worldwide – those with the smallest proportion remaining in a nearly natural condition – are those of fresh waters, wetlands, coral reefs, oceanic islands, Mediterranean-climate areas, temperate rain forests, temperate grasslands and tropical dry forests. Although there are still large areas remaining, tropical moist forests in many regions are being cleared at a fast rate wherever they occur. Because tropical moist forests are believed to hold at least half of the world's species, their continuing destruction will cause the biggest losses.

Right Elephant hunters caught by an anti-poaching patrol in Luangwa National Park, Zambia. Poaching for ivory promises rewards only because foreign buyers are prepared to pay large sums for illegally taken animal products. Poaching is now the greatest threat to the survival of the African elephant.

Below Hardwood logs are trimmed and prepared for export from Congo, Central Africa. Tropical rainforests provide excellent timber for construction and furniture. In their eagerness to reap the benefits of this resource, many countries have allowed unsustainable commercial logging operations.

salinization, are also ruining large areas of soil. Logging in tropical forests is rarely undertaken on a sustainable basis, greatly reducing the productivity and diversity of 44,000 square kilometres (15,000 square miles) each year.

Most marine fisheries are exploited at levels close to or beyond their capacities for renewal. Many stocks in the north-west Atlantic were heavily overfished in the late 1960s, and catches remain a fraction of their former size. Excessive hunting of many fur-bearing mammals, of rhinoceroses for their horn, of crocodiles for their hide and of turtles for their meat and shell has brought many species close to extinction and necessitated bans on their trade. If exploitation had been sustainable, it could have given some people secure livelihoods and provided long-term economic benefits.

In the drive to maximize short-term gains, our use of biological resources is not sustainable

To conserve the vitality and diversity of the biosphere, both in its own right and as an essential foundation for human development, key actions are needed to prevent pollution, restore and maintain the integrity of the Earth's ecosystems, conserve biological diversity and ensure that renewable resources are used sustainably. Just as the various issues overlap, so positive efforts to deal with them are closely interlinked.

Renewable resources

Biological resources – the species and ecosystems on which we rely for food and other natural products – are renewable only if utilized sustainably. That means maintaining their stocks and not undermining their long-term productivity. It means conserving soils and soil fertility, and harvesting timber without impairing the growth of replacement trees or degrading the forest ecosystem. It means fishing without causing catches to decline and reducing the level of hunting and trapping if a target animal starts to become scarce. The results of unsustainable use (as well as damage to biodiversity and life-support systems) are shortages in supply and economic loss. Unfortunately, in the drive to maximize short-term gains, much of our use of biological resources is not sustainable.

Every year, soil erosion renders 60–70,000 square kilometres (20–25,000 square miles) of farm land useless for cultivation – more than twice the rate in the past three centuries. Badly managed irrigation schemes, leading to waterlogging and

Tackling pollution

Pollution has grown from a local nuisance to a global menace, demanding action by governments, municipalities and industries in all countries. Many potential dangers of pollution are not as yet fully understood. Limiting emissions of gases that might contribute to global warming, protecting river systems and preventing the pollution of the sea are of high priority. Special attention should also be given to sewage treatment, to minimizing the run-off of fertilizers and livestock wastes from farmland, and to curbing the discharge of persistent organic substances and heavy metals.

Upper-income countries must intensify their efforts to clean up existing emissions. Lower-income countries should ensure they do not create future problems by accepting new industrial development that emits excessive pollution. One of the most effective changes that can be made is to create a single pollution authority, with adequate powers and resources to control discharges to air, rivers and the sea, and the disposal of solid wastes.

Such integrated pollution control avoids the risk that polluting materials will simply be transferred from one medium to another. The same agency should have the power to set effluent standards for vehicles, and control the use of chemicals in agricultural and household products.

In setting regulations and providing economic incentives for reduced emissions, governments can be guided by the Polluter Pays Principle (in parallel with the User Pays Principle, see page 39). This principle requires that market prices reflect the full costs of environmental damage.

A mine or a chemical factory, for example, should pay the costs of ensuring that its effluents and emissions do not damage fisheries or create a hazard to health if they are polluting the ocean. The result is that a strong incentive for pollution control is created, thus encouraging industries to develop new processes, consumer goods that do not release pollutants, and better techniques for reclaiming useful or hazardous materials.

Ecosystem management

Protecting ecosystems and the life-support services they provide from destruction and disruption requires a broad outlook – one that goes beyond individual sites. Drainage basins are the natural units for land use management, since water links different ecosystems and activities upstream inevitably have an impact downstream. The economic value attached to each basin's ecosystems should recognize their role in regulating water quality and quantity. Peat swamp forest in Malaysia is being conserved because it is known to provide a reliable source of water during the dry season for nearby rice fields. Experience has shown that draining swamps and building reservoirs as substitutes for natural water storage is costly and unsatisfactory.

To maintain life-support services overall, each region needs to preserve or restore as much of its natural and modified ecosystems as possible (see box opposite). Conversion from one condition to another should always be thoroughly questioned.

Forests are particularly important as resources, as reservoirs of biodiversity and as absorbers of atmospheric carbon. Where their conversion is essential it should be compensated by the restoration of forests in other areas, and in their exploitation, excessive or destructive harvesting should always be avoided. Successful forest restoration projects have been established in India where families living in the fringes of degraded forest have agreed to protect, help rehabilitate and maintain the forest in return for forest-based employment and the rights to collect fuelwood and fodder and

sell forest products. Nearly 1,800 of such Forest Protection Committees have now been organized, and they protect close to 21,000 square kilometres (8,000 square miles) of forest land.

The maintenance of modified ecosystems is equally important within farmed and urbanized landscapes. Action should be taken to preserve small areas of wetland, woodland and species-rich meadows, as well as to maintain parks and gardens, especially those in which native species of plant and tree are growing.

Pollution has grown from a local nuisance to a global menace

Above A spectacular sunset over the Patanal, a vast wetland in western Brazil fed by seasonal flooding and long used for cattle ranching. Although the Patanal faces some problems of habitat change, hunting and pressure from tourism, it is a natural haven where cattle can co-exist with abundant wildlife.

Left Pollution in the North Sea has produced unsightly foam along a stretch of the Dutch coastline. Obviously, unnatural, this foam is a manifestation of widespread pollution. Loaded with varied wastes and toxins, the productivity of many marine ecosystems has become increasingly diminshed.

Classification of ecosystem conditions

Ecosystems can be divided into five categories, based on their prevailing conditions.

• Natural systems: ecosystems where human impact, first, has been no greater than that of any other species and, second, has not affected the ecosystem's structure.

• Modified systems: ecosystems where human impact is greater than that of any other species, but whose structural components are not cultivated, for example, naturally regenerating forest that is used for timber extraction or natural grassland used for pasture.

• Cultivated systems: ecosystems where most of the structural components are cultivated, such as arable farmland, sown pasture, tree plantations or aquaculture ponds.

• Built systems: ecosystems dominated by buildings, roads, railways, ports, dams, mines and other human structures.

• Degraded systems: ecosystems whose diversity, productivity and habitability have been substantially reduced. Degraded land ecosystems are characterized by loss of vegetation and soil. Degraded aquatic ecosystems often have severely polluted water.

Uses of an ecosystem are sustainable if the system can be maintained without serious change. Unsustainable uses lead to conversion of part or all of the ecosystem to some lower condition – for example, from a natural system to a modified system. Living sustainably calls for protection of natural systems; sustainable production of wild renewable resources from modified systems; sustainable production of crops and livestock from cultivated systems; development of built systems in ways that are sensitive to human and ecological communities; and the restoration or rehabilitation of degraded systems.

Conserving biodiversity

Biological diversity should be conserved by measures for preserving both ecosystems and individually threatened species. Networks of protected areas, of which there are many kinds (see box on this page) are the most effective single measure. They range from strict nature reserves to managed resource areas where conservation is geared to sustained production of water, timber or pasture.

Every nation needs a comprehensive system of protected areas, but without adequate resources a system can become little more than a list on paper. Already, protected areas have been degraded in many countries, and priority should be given to their restoration. Conservation agencies need the tools and resources for management, trained staff and sufficient funds.

It is important to take account of the likely impact of future climate change. To maintain diversity in the long term, systems must allow for changes in the distribution of species by protecting the full range of environments and ensuring that protected areas are linked by corridors of suitable habitat along which species can migrate.

Saving species

Many species can be conserved simply by management of their habitats in protected areas. However, others, especially the large and commercially valuable species, often require more intensive care, including protection from hunters, relocation to secure refuges and veterinary help. Many countries lack the expertise for such management. Their conservation agencies need adequate resources and well-trained staff in fields such as animal capture, disease control and eradication of harmful non-native animals and plants. Special anti-poaching schemes, always involving local people, may be necessary to protect some endangered species.

The highest priority is the conservation of species in their natural habitats (in situ). However, where habitats have become so degraded or populations have fallen so low that survival in the wild cannot be guaranteed, conservation through breeding and propagation in captivity (ex situ), often in zoological or botanical gardens, may be necessary. Reintroduction of captive-bred individuals to the wild may be possible in future. Conservation is also important for wild relatives of domesticated animals and crop plants, and for races of domesticated species that are in danger of being lost.

Knowledge of the status and distribution of many animal and plant species, especially in tropical countries, is still poor. Regional and international co-operation in research and surveys is vital to ensure that the best possible decisions are made.

Functions of protected areas

A system of protected areas is the core of any programme that seeks to maintain the diversity of ecosystems and species; and to protect the world's great natural areas for their intrinsic, inspirational and recreational values. Protected areas can also have many more tangible benefits for development when they:

• Conserve soil and water in zones that are highly erodible if the original vegetation is removed
• Regulate and purify water flow, notably by protecting wetlands and forests
• Shield people from natural disasters (for example, coral reefs, mangroves and coastal wetlands provide natural barriers against storm surges)
• Maintain wild genetic resources or species important in medicine
• Provide a suitable habitat for harvested species
• Permit the sustainable use of wild resources in modified ecosystems
• Provide employment, notably from tourism.

Sustainable harvesting

Harvests of biological resources need to be regulated if they are to be sustainable. This requires better knowledge of the productive capacities of resources through research and monitoring, and regulation to keep exploitation well within the limits. This can be done by controlling access or by setting harvest quotas. For fisheries, for instance, this can mean limiting the number and size of fishing boats and the duration of the open season, or granting rights to catch only a specific quantity of fish, the sum of individual quotas being no more than the estimated sustainable yield of the stock. Where there are competing claims on the resource, local needs should generally have priority over external commercial and recreational uses.

Incentives to use natural resources sustainably depend on the property rights of users. People with exclusive or long-term rights to a resource are more likely to limit their harvests to conserve the resource. For example, someone whose rights to graze livestock extend far into the future has an incentive to manage the rangeland for continued productivity, whereas a grazier whose rights are limited to one season does not. Local communities should be granted secure land tenure and property rights, especially indigenous peoples and other groups with a long attachment to a particular area.

Economic return to local communities from the use of resources is important. Those that successfully conserve stocks should be allowed to export the sustainable surplus or develop other ways to gain revenue from it. The Irula of southern India, for example, traditionally relied upon the snakeskin trade, but by 1972 snakes had become so scarce that the trade was shut down. However, the Irula were permitted to milk venom from wild snakes and then release them. The venom is used to make anti-snakebite serum and other drugs. Continued by a co-operative with a membership of 150, venom collection has filled the income gap that was left by the ending of the skin trade. The snake population is no longer declining and people earn more per snake than when they hunted them.

Left In traditional manner, a fisherman sets out across Lake Dali in China. Such fishing practices that have been practised for centuries generally harvest fish sustainably, that is, they do not take fish at a rate greater than that at which the fish can replenish themselves. A lake provides a simple model for the global fishing industry: if we harvest too many fish today, then there will be no fish tomorrow.

Left Hoar frost, cloud and mountains in the Wolong Nature Reserve, Sichuan, China. When we preserve a natural ecosystem, we not only protect its biodiversity, we also conserve the extraordinary natural beauty of our planet.

Above At a government Wildlife Unit in Zimbabwe, a trained technical assistant helps care for young ostrich chicks. By offering timely veterinary intervention, such Wildlife Units can help preserve the health of wild animal populations and protect them against disease.

Priority Actions

1 Adopt a precautionary approach to pollution

All societies should adopt the precautionary principles of minimizing discharges of substances that could be harmful and of ensuring that products and processes are non-polluting. Efforts are needed by:

• Governments in all countries, to tackle pollution in an integrated manner, employing a mix of economic and regulatory measures

• Municipalities and public utilities, to maintain or improve air quality in their areas and bring sewage treatment up to modern standards

• Industries, to make use of the best available technology and design to prevent pollution

• Farmers, to use agrochemicals sparingly and minimize run-off of fertilizers and livestock wastes from agricultural land

• Domestic consumers, to dispose of household waste carefully, not pour hazardous chemicals into waste water systems and minimize the use of chemical insecticides in the garden.

2 Adopt an integrated approach to land and water management

All uses of land and water within a drainage basin may affect water quality and flow, and hence have an impact on other uses and ecosystems downstream. To avoid this:

• Governments and their agencies, especially integrated pollution control agencies, and water, agriculture and forestry authorities, should use drainage basins as the natural units for land and water management

• Development of water resources should be integrated with maintenance of ecosystems that play an essential role in the water cycle, such as watershed forests and wetlands.

3 Maintain as much as possible of natural and modified ecosystems

Recognizing the pressing need for protection of life-support systems, biodiversity and renewable resources, each country should:

• Preserve remaining natural ecosystems, unless there are overwhelming reasons for change to be necessary

• Work out ways of using such ecosystems sustainably, thus improving their economic and social value

• Maintain as large an area as possible of modified ecosystems that support a variety of sustainable uses and a diversity of natural species

• Halt net deforestation, protect large areas of undisturbed forest and maintain a permanent estate of modified forest

• Take the pressure off natural and modified systems by protecting the best farmland, preventing soil degradation and enhancing its long-term productivity by sustainable means

• Take the full social costs and benefits into account when converting land to agriculture and urban systems

• Encourage land occupiers and local communities to maintain as much diversity as possible within these systems, by preserving wild areas, raising diverse crops and planting native plants

• Restore or rehabilitate ecosystems that have become degraded.

Above A visitor information map at W National Park, Niger. It is essential that all countries establish protected areas for the survival of our planet's ecosystems and biodiversity. Properly managed, such areas can also be valuable sources of revenue.

Above right At a coastal settlement near Karachi, Pakistan, villagers carry a green turtle back to the ocean. The support and participation of local residents and communities are very important elements in the implementation of plans to protect species and ecosystems.

4
Establish a comprehensive network of protected areas

Every country needs a national system of protected areas. There should be an overall plan setting out the objectives of the system, its coverage of habitat types and a timetable for filling in gaps. The system should be governed by an explicit policy that:
• Ensures each protected area has an up-to-date management plan which is effectively implemented
• Ensures the participation of local communities in the design, management and operation of protected areas
• Maintains a sustainable economic return from protected areas but makes sure that much of this goes to manage the area and reaches local communities
• Encourages local, especially indigenous, communities and private organizations to establish and manage protected areas
• Ensures that the system safeguards the full range of national ecosystem and species diversity.

5
Improve conservation of wild species

Each country should do all it can to prevent species extinction. Threatened species should be restored to safe levels and non-threatened ones should not be allowed to decline significantly. Important actions should include:
• Implementation of national and international recovery plans for threatened species
• Development of techniques to manage small populations of species, taking account of the need to prevent inbreeding and local extinction by accidents, ecological hazards and climate change
• Strict measures to prevent the release into the wild of non-native species of animals, plants and pathogens
• Improvement of techniques to eliminate the illegal taking of plants and animals
• Adherence to the Convention on Trade in Endangered Species (CITES) and strong action to improve its effectiveness
• Close integration between ex situ and in situ programmes
• Management of captive populations to ensure they do not require continuous addition of wild specimens
• In captive breeding, emphasis on benefits to threatened species and avoidance of commercial transactions.

6
Harvest wild resources sustainably

In most countries, wild species and uncultivated ecosystems are an important resource. Management of them for sustainable use requires:
• An ability to assess stocks and productive capacities of exploited ecosystems, and to ensure that use and harvesting keep within those capacities
• Establishment of harvest limits that allow for ignorance and uncertainty about the biology of harvested species, the condition of the ecosystem, and other impacts on the species and ecosystem
• Conservation of the habitats and ecosystems that support the resource.

7
Support management of renewable resources by local communities

Resources are best conserved if local communities take part in decisions about their management and local people have exclusive and long-term rights to their use. Therefore:
• Governments and local communities should jointly develop policy for renewable resource management
• Local communities should be granted secure land tenure and property rights and be encouraged to develop strong community institutions
• Communities that successfully conserve wildlife stocks should be enabled to export the sustainable surplus and receive the revenues earned
• Combinations of economic incentives can promote conservation by local communities, including direct returns such as shares of entrance fees to a protected area.

Energy Use and Efficiency

Energy from the Sun warms and lights our environment. It is absorbed by plants, which convert it into sugars and starches stored in their tissues, which we in turn absorb with the plant and animal food we eat. Thus it is ultimately the Sun's energy that powers our muscles and all of our other bodily functions. However, many thousands of years ago, humans began to exploit forms of energy from "new", secondary sources.

The first new source of energy was fire – used to provide heat in dwellings, cook food and shape tools. For a long time, wood and dung were the main sources of this energy, and in some regions they were the only fuels. Later people began to harness the draught power of cattle and horses, the power of wind captured by sails and windmills, and the power of water to turn waterwheels. The mechanical energy delivered by windmills and waterwheels, and the heat energy released by wood after its conversion to charcoal, were the first forms of energy used for industrial purposes.

Above **A woman cooks the daily meal on the Carari reservation, Amazonia, Brazil. The fuel for the fire and the meat for the pot were both taken from the surrounding rainforest. Traditional use of fuelwood can be sustainable, but in many parts of the world rising populations stretch the supply beyond its capacity for regeneration.**

From 1950 to 1970, total energy consumption rose by 5.2 per cent per year

Some simple societies are still driven by human and animal power and fuelled by wood, charcoal and dung. But in industrial societies, energy requirements – and hence fuel production and use – have become much more sophisticated. In these countries, commercial energy consumption has grown at a continually accelerating rate.

Nuclear waste

Originally hailed as a cheap, clean substitute for fossil-fuels, nuclear power has been dogged by concerns over its safety. Concerns arise over the fear of accident, elevated after the disaster at Chernobyl, and from the fact that no nation has so far demonstrated that dangerous wastes arising from the industry can be securely and safely disposed of. By the year 2000, the cumulative amount of high-level waste (including spent fuel from nuclear reactors) produced worldwide could have reached 1 million cubic metres (1.3 million cubic yards). Regardless of the future for the industry, finding ways of securely disposing of such wastes should no longer be delayed.

Below Nuclear waste is loaded aboard a ship for disposal at sea. The problem of disposing of radioactive waste from nuclear power plants has yet to be solved, with grave doubts cast over the safety of the methods used today and those proposed for the future.

Rising demands

A turning point in energy production and use began with the development of steam power based on the combustion of coal. Steam power was soon used to drive several different types of engine for a wide range of industrial uses, as well as for land and water transportation. This increasing number of applications, coupled with the rising demands of growing populations for a host of products, led to a phenomenal increase in energy use.

During the nineteenth century, steam power was complemented by that from internal combustion engines, powered by fossil fuels, and electricity generators based on fossil fuels or water power. This century, the importance of fossil fuels has been overwhelming, with their products serving the engines of most forms of transport, and cabled electricity being supplied to buildings at the flick of a switch. These uses have spread with varying intensity to all countries of the world.

Energy demands and production have grown year by year throughout the course of the twentieth century. From 1950 to 1970, total energy consumption rose by 5.2 per cent per year to the equivalent of nearly 6 billion tonnes of oil; today, the figure is around 10 billion tonnes. As the demand grew, so did the transport and transmission of energy. Fossil fuels came to be exported all over the world from producing countries. Cables on pylons and buried underground spread out in ever more complicated networks from power stations to serve the myriad electricity consumers.

Energy sources

Since the mid-twentieth century, some electricity has been generated by atomic fission, but widescale adoption of nuclear power has been slowed by fear of accident and by uncertainty about the disposal of radioactive waste (see box on this page). Globally, nuclear power is still less important than hydroelectric power.

Other forms of energy supply include electricity generation from wind, wave and tidal power, and from the subterranean heat of the Earth (geothermal power), direct use of sunlight for heating, and alternative fuels, such as ethanol processed from sugar cane for vehicles. There have been many local small-scale successes in developing such sources of energy as alternatives to more conventional sources. These have included the fitting of solar collector panels for domestic heating and the creation of "wind farms" using ranks of wind turbines for electricity generation. So far, however, they have made little contribution worldwide, and fossil fuels continue to provide the bulk of commercial energy.

Energy issues

Commercial energy is essential for development. It is no accident that the countries that use very little are among the poorest in the world. However, commercial energy production also raises a large number of major environmental issues. Energy facilities, such as coal mines, oil-drilling platforms, dams and power stations, are generally large and visually intrusive. They compete with other forms of land use and degrade natural ecosystems, often to the point of complete destruction. Pollution in various forms is a by-product of most stages in the cycle of production, transmission, transport and use of energy. Today's biggest energy-production industries are steadily using up the non-renewable resources on which they depend. This is particularly the case with the fossil fuel industries, and here there is also the problem that their resources are set to be of increasing value in the future as raw materials for many parts of the chemical industry, such as plastics and pharmaceuticals.

Our dependence on fossil fuels and the ways we use them lie at the heart of many energy-related environmental problems. Oil, coal and, to a lesser extent, gas create various kinds of pollution during extraction, transportation and combustion in heating systems, engines and power stations. Mining wastes contaminate soil and acidify surface waters. Oil spills and leakages from off-shore installations and tanker ships cause marine pollution. The burning of fossil fuels generates air pollutants including sulphur dioxide, nitrogen oxides and carbon dioxide, and is the principal contributor to global warming. Renewable energy sources, by contrast, are not exhaustible and tend to produce less or virtually no pollution. But set against this are considerable technological problems in harnessing them. Furthermore, no energy source, however clean, can be exploited without there being some environmental impact. Hydroelectric power schemes, for example, involve building dams and flooding large areas, which may displace communities and conflict with the conservation of landscapes and biological diversity. Wind, wave and solar power all require installations that may affect habitats or amenities.

Not only is it proving difficult to harness the potential of alternative energy sources, but we are also using up more of the conventional sources than we need to. There is much waste in the commercial energy industry and in the use of its products – wastage that also serves to exacerbate levels of pollution. For example, electrical heating systems make use of high-grade heat from fuel combustion to produce low-grade heat, that is, to make the temperature of rooms only a few degrees different from that of the adjacent environment. Many power stations shed waste heat into their environment as hot water, steam or warm air. Only quite recently have combined heat and power plants been developed to market their low-grade heat to warm nearby buildings. Many buildings are poorly insulated, wasting money and energy through the avoidable leakage of heat into the surrounding air in cool weather, and leading to overheated working conditions in hot weather. Many industrial processes still use far more energy than is needed to power the operations they undertake. Motor vehicles consume about one third of the oil used in the world and some 40 per cent of all the energy used in upper-income countries. They are notoriously inefficient as well as being major sources of pollution.

**There is much waste in
the commercial energy industry
and in the use of its products**

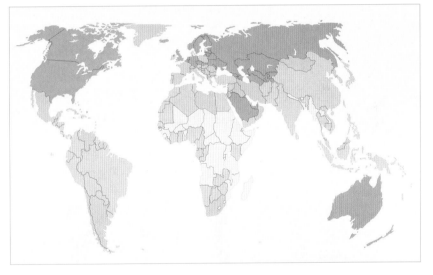

Left A geothermal power station at Olkaria, Kenya. Such a plant has little impact on the environment: it does not use non-renewable resources and produces no pollution. Unfortunately, there are a limited number of suitable sites in the world.

Below left An open-pit coal mine in Zimbabwe, owned by an international company that may have little concern for the environment of the local people. Apart from the pollution caused by burning fossil fuels, their extraction can have severe impacts.

Below The map shows the energy consumption for each country expressed as the equivalent to kilograms of coal consumed per person in 1989. (Separate statistics for the republics of the former Soviet Union and Yugoslavia are not available.)

Controlling consumption

If society is to progress towards sustainability, control of energy consumption is vital. Improving the efficiency with which we generate and consume energy will not only help safeguard supplies, but also it will reduce pollution and minimize the conversion of additional land to energy production and transmission. It has been calculated that steady progress in cutting energy demand could reduce carbon dioxide emissions in several high-income countries by between 1 and 2 per cent per year. On this basis, the United States could readily cut its emissions by 60 per cent by the year 2050.

Recently, energy efficiency has been improving steadily in many high-income countries, largely stimulated by increases in world oil prices. But it has been declining in several newly industrializing countries. Too frequently, growth in energy consumption has been treated as a yardstick of economic growth, regardless of the efficiency with which that energy has been used. Many countries actually subsidize energy for the consumer, reducing the incentive for careful use. We need to decouple economic growth from growth in energy production, and recognize that if we are to achieve sustainability we must achieve the first without a matching expansion in the second. Both the energy-generation industry and the consumer should be charged in full for their use of fossil fuels, with appropriate taxes to ensure that prices match their true costs to society.

In all countries, an important step is to develop a long-term energy strategy that sets targets for energy efficiency and lays out environmental guidelines for all sectors of the energy industry. Planning should commence with an analysis of human needs and a consideration of how these can be met most efficiently and equitably. Citizens' groups, especially environmental NGOs, and business and industry should be fully involved in the development of the strategy. In line with the strategy, national environmental protection agencies should be given responsibility for setting energy efficiency standards and monitoring their attainment by industry, and conservation guidelines should be provided for energy users.

Energy Consumption

	Under 100 kg
	100-1,000 kg
	1000-5,000 kg
	5000-10,000 kg
	Over 10,000 kg

Practices and technology

Reducing wastage in energy production and transmission depends partly on changing practices, such as preventing the routine leakage of fuel from badly maintained pipelines and gearing electricity generation to fluctuations in demand. It also requires use of the best available technology. The latest generation of gas turbines, for example, has increased the efficiency of conversion of heat to electricity in power stations from 33 per cent to about 50 per cent.

Improving the efficiency of energy use by the consumer also requires both changes in established practices and technical improvements. Reducing energy demand includes changing behaviour: for example, doing more work at home to reduce vehicle use and ensuring that lighting is switched on only when needed. In many countries, about half the commercial energy supplied is used to heat the space in which people live and work. Such heating is often highly inefficient, but could easily be improved by better insulation and better use of the thermostat. Energy-saving technology in industrial processes has successfully cut consumption in some steel and chemical works.

Doubling the fuel efficiency of cars to an average of about 20 kilometres per litre (80 miles per US gallon/100 miles per Imperial gallon) would halve the amount of carbon dioxide (about 500 million tonnes) that the world's 400 million cars emit to the atmosphere annually. This performance standard could already be met by present technology, and could be doubled in future.

Energy-efficient technology can also be applied in communities far from the bustle of industrialized society. In rural areas of lower-income countries, stoves that use kerosene, liquid petroleum gas or electricity instead of wood or charcoal can perform as well using 30 per cent of the energy and avoiding the environmental degradation caused by excessive use of fuelwood. However, assistance may be needed to make the higher quality fuels available to the poor.

Technology can be used more widely to clean up some of the emissions from energy consumption. Catalytic converters reduce the output of noxious exhaust gases from petrol-driven vehicles, while desulphurization equipment in smoke stacks can remove up to 95 per cent of the sulphur dioxide released by fossil-fuel burning power stations.

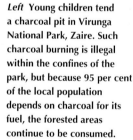

Left Young children tend a charcoal pit in Virunga National Park, Zaire. Such charcoal burning is illegal within the confines of the park, but because 95 per cent of the local population depends on charcoal for its fuel, the forested areas continue to be consumed.

Above A coal-fired power station near Cologne, Germany, pours smoke and steam into the atmosphere. There are polluting chemicals in the smoke, and the steam carries unused heat, which wastes a non-renewable resource, coal, and thus increases pollution.

Right A poster shows the causes of acid rain and what will be damaged if the levels of pollution that cause it continue. There will not be significant improvement in energy efficiency without support from consumers: campaigning and education are therefore essential.

Support for change

To succeed, energy policies need the widest possible support. The drive to energy efficiency cannot go ahead without the co-operation of consumers. Information campaigns are vital to promote necessary changes. They should make use of all media, extend into environmental education in schools and include demonstrations of successful practice.

Because of the global aspects of energy-related issues, such as climate change, global action is appropriate. International co-operation, including development aid, should include exchanges of knowledge about technology, and help with the transfer of technology to developing countries. Development assistance agencies and development banks could switch their emphasis from funding conventional energy projects to providing more help for renewable energy projects and for measures to improve efficiency and conservation.

Sources and priorities

A choice of energy source can also go a long way to relieving some environmental ills. Alternative renewable sources hold out promise, and governments should support continued research and development work to make them more viable. Advances such as the development of photovoltaic cells, which convert sunlight directly into electric current, are already proving efficient for small-scale installations. But, at least for the time being, society will have to make informed choices between conventional sources.

A well-designed system for taxing energy could encourage a switch to those sources that emit less carbon dioxide and other pollutants. The cleanest source of energy should be taxed only enough to achieve efficiency, while other sources should be taxed at progressively higher rates to deter pollution. Taxes on fossil fuels would, for this reason, be high for coal, moderate for oil and low for natural gas. Most coal burning emits between 70 and 95 per cent more carbon dioxide than gas per unit of useful energy produced. Oil is intermediate, producing 35-45 per cent more than gas.

At present, many nations favour the use of indigenous fossil fuels, especially coal, even when this is unduly costly or brings needless environmental impact. While self-reliance may be a legitimate goal, total self-sufficiency often makes neither economic nor environmental sense.

Priority Actions

1
Develop explicit national energy strategies

Each government should prepare a national strategy for its commercial energy industries, covering extraction, conversion, transport and use for the next 30 years. It should include:
• Policies for the optimal use of fossil fuel resources, with explicit statements of the technical and economic means that will be used to reduce consumption, wastage and pollution
• Policies for the development and safe use of other energy sources
• Policies and standards for the energy efficiency of processes and products, including vehicles
• Economic policies to ensure that the price of energy covers the full social cost of its production, distribution and use
• Use of taxes or incentives to encourage greater energy efficiency in homes, and to shelter the poorer sectors of society from the impact of increases in energy prices that these policies may cause.

2
Rationalize power generation from fossil fuels

Governments should promote economy and pollution reduction in the use of fossil fuels by:
• Imposing standards of fuel-use efficiency on the energy-generating industries; the standards should be based on use of the best available technology
• Setting standards for acceptable loss of energy or fuel in distribution, and requiring that losses above that standard be charged against the profits of the industry rather than to the consumer
• Setting standards for pollution emissions; the standards should be based on use of the best available technology.

3
Develop renewable and other non-fossil fuel energy sources

Research and development related to the use of renewable energy sources must continue. Governments should support this work, and exchange the results through international bodies such as the International Energy Agency. Development aid agencies should help. Key elements in their policies should be:
• Increased use of hydropower, particularly small-scale installations, but only where Environmental Impact Assessment (EIA) shows the development to be truly cost-effective
• Promotion of the development and use of geothermal, wind and wave energy, again in localities suited to them, and only following EIA for each development
• Promotion of small-scale solar energy systems (photovoltaic cells) for use in domestic situations and to power individual installations like pumps
• Encouragement of simple technology that uses solar energy directly for heating and drying
• Continued development of biomass-based fuels where they can be derived from crop residues, surpluses or crops from land not needed for food growing
• Use of methane emitted from decomposing waste in landfill sites for energy generation or heating
• Investment in research into possible fuel systems for the future, for example, based on hydrogen
• Continued pursuit of a cautious policy regarding nuclear power, concentrating on safe and efficient operation of stations.

5
Conduct publicity campaigns to promote energy conservation

Governments, citizens' groups and industry should promote energy conservation and efficiency:

• Drawing attention to and explaining energy efficiency information given on consumer products and in the sales details of such things as vehicles and appliances, so that people understand them and can make informed choices

• Devising award schemes that give prominence to new energy-conserving devices, and rewarding companies or groups whose performance has been outstanding in this area

• Explaining and demonstrating how energy-efficiency audits should be carried out, and explaining how savings can be made in buildings such as schools, offices and factories

• Explaining the reasons why energy prices are being raised, and publicizing how those most disadvantaged and in need can get help.

4
Use energy more efficiently in the home, industry, business and transport

There is immense scope for saving energy and money through greater efficiency in the ways we consume fuel and power. It is a process to which millions of people can contribute. Actions should include the following:

• Enforcing standards for energy efficiency in industry, space heating, building construction and transport

• Carrying out energy audits in public, commercial and industrial premises, to show where significant energy savings can be made

• The development of energy-efficient vehicles and aircraft, improvement of public transport and reduced dependence on the private car, ensuring that each means of transport is charged its full cost to the community

• Clearly stating the energy efficiency of all electric appliances and vehicles on the product or in the sales details

• Improving energy conservation in buildings, for example, by insulation and draught excluders, and by lighting and heating rooms only when they are in use

• The use of more efficient cooking stoves, particularly in areas hitherto dependent on fuelwood.

Left Unwanted gas being burned-off at the El-Borma oil field in southern Tunisia. Although this field has only small reserves, the gas – which can be used as fuel – is wasted in the hurry to satisfy the demand for oil.

Above left Wind turbines crowd the skyline outside the desert resort of Palm Springs, California. Wind turbines produce no pollution, but they have a high visual impact and are noisy for nearby residents.

Above Solar-cell powered vehicles taking part in a competition in Switzerland. Events such as this help to bring alternative energy use into the public eye, as well as providing good opportunities for experimentation.

Industry and Commerce

Business is of paramount importance in our lives. Industry (the extraction, harvesting or conversion of raw materials, the fabrication of new objects or mechanisms, and the transportation of commodities and manufactured goods) and commerce (the trade in goods and services) together comprise all the activities people undertake with the intention of producing and selling goods and services. It is they that create economies, knit societies together and improve our material standards of living. But industry and commerce also have the potential to damage the environment in which they exist, and on which they ultimately depend.

The beginnings of business lay in the handicrafts and barter of prehistory. Skills in fabricating beautiful and useful objects and mechanisms from plant and animal fibres, woods, stone and metals were passed from one generation to the next and became increasingly sophisticated. Very early on it was recognized that there were advantages in accumulating goods for later use or for trade, and in agreeing on some single, durable commodity to represent units of value and serve as a medium of exchange. Thus was money born.

As skills were further developed, more knowledge accumulated and better methods of production devised, the quantity and quality of goods increased. Facilitated by the use of money, more and more goods and commodities were traded in local and regional markets.

The first large businesses were probably associated with agriculture: activities such as managing the production and distribution of large quantities of grain in the valleys of the rivers Nile, Tigris-Euphrates and Indus, and of the great rivers of China. Converting the natural flood plains and adjacent areas from marshes and grasslands with a rich native flora and fauna to irrigated fields and managed pastures caused a significant ecological impact. So did the deforestation of the mountains of Greece and the gradual clearance of the woodlands of western and central Europe. During much of the period of these developments, activities such as smelting, metal working, dyeing and tanning would have caused severe but localized pollution.

Revolution in industry

The Industrial Revolution at the turn of the nineteenth century transformed every aspect of industry including the nature of its inputs, outputs and conversion processes. Above all, it changed the input of energy from mainly animal and water power to that derived from fossil fuels. The manufacture of new chemicals, and of a great many new products, often yielded unwanted by-products, or wastes, which, through ignorance or indifference, were disposed of as cheaply as possible without considering their effects on the environment or human health. Today, the consequences of waste disposal cannot escape attention in the light of the vastly increased concentrations of human populations, the much greater levels of industrial activity, the burgeoning numbers of harmful chemicals regularly found in industrial waste and better scientific understanding of environmental sensitivity.

The Industrial Revolution vastly expanded the volume of trade throughout the world, extended trade routes and forged great changes in transportation and communication.

Above Agricultural produce being loaded at a Brazilian port. The world's five billion people generate staggering volumes of trade, and individual ships can now carry over 300,000 ton(ne)s of cargo. The development of transport has been a key factor in the advance of industry and increase in trade. Many problems, including the consumption of great amounts of energy, pollution of air and water, and economic disparity are the result of world trade conditions and practices.

Above A banana truck outside Karachi, Pakistan. For lower-income countries, cash crops for export such as bananas may seem attractive for earning foreign currency, but they can become an economic millstone. The market is fickle, and glut is far more common than shortage. A district can find that it is geared to producing an unwanted crop.

Right A trail of sludge lying in the wake of a ship that is dumping it at sea as a cheap method of disposal. Although such practices may save money for the those responsible for the dumping, the environmental costs are often considerable. Marine dumping can be difficult to police, and a combination of controls and incentives are required to prevent it.

Motor vehicles have also had a huge impact on the environment and on human health. They emit many pollutants, particularly carbon dioxide, carbon monoxide, oxides of nitrogen, hydrocarbons and smoke – and in some countries they still emit small quantities of lead, which is added to fuel to improve engine performance. The manufacture of vehicles requires large quantities of metals, plastics, fabrics and energy, while the transportation of their fuel is the cause of a significant degree of marine pollution. Very large amounts of space are occupied by highways and parking lots and the noise created by vehicles can be severely detrimental to the quality of life.

During the past 40 years or so, aircraft have become a highly important means of transport and are now the major carriers of intercontinental and other long-distance passengers. They also transport increasingly large volumes of high-value, low-weight freight. Many of the environmental impacts of aircraft are similar to those of ground vehicles: they use materials and fuels, emit pollutants to the atmosphere and are responsible for significant noise pollution, especially in areas near to airports.

Motor vehicles dominate our economies and have a tremendous impact on the environment

First came changes in inland tranport with the construction of canal and railway networks. Then came the change from small ships driven by the wind to large carriers powered by steam. The object of these technological advances was the need or desire to move commodities and goods in two directions: raw materials such as iron ore, lumber and coffee beans from their sources to the centres of manufacturing; and finished products such as sewing machines, books and furniture out to the markets for sale.

The next, and perhaps the greatest change in transportation came with the invention of the internal combustion engine: a small, light-weight motor that is driven by an easily handled and relatively cheap, liquid fuel. The motor vehicle in the form of automobile, bus or truck is now the major means of transporting people and facilitating their communication, and of carrying trade goods and commodities throughout the world. It has also become a dominant force in the economies of most high-income countries. It has had a deep influence on social values, customs and life styles, not least in both creating and satisfying an unprecedented demand for travel and recreation.

Services and capital

Patterns of human activity are continually changing, and have done so at an unprecedentedly rapid rate during the twentieth century. Centres of industrial manufacture first sprang up in Europe and North America, but have now spread to many other parts of the world. At the same time, service industries, such as retailing, finance, information, health care, travel, tourism and accommodation, have greatly expanded.

Service industries generally have less direct environmental impact than the industries that convert materials and produce goods and wastes. However, many of the service industries, such as retailing, travel and accommodation, are dependent upon one or another of the extractive or manufacturing industries and thus have a direct influence on the volumes and patterns of industrial production. Some industries, such as health care and photographic services, produce small volumes of highly hazardous wastes and must therefore be very carefully managed.

All business requires capital. Even the smallest modern enterprise needs a substantial investment at the outset. In Italy during the Renaissance, an elaborate system emerged for trading money and credit, for using the capital accumulated through one venture in trade or manufacture to start up another. From small beginnings, banking has since extended to become global in its operations, supported by vast accumulations of capital yielded by the world economy. The resulting flows of money and credit have a major influence on decisions affecting the environment.

The development and environmental impacts of industry and commerce have not been evenly distributed throughout the world. The evolution of business has been such that manufacturing and capital are concentrated in the developed countries. Despite the global span of the banking business, its control remains with a few major institutions in those countries. On the other hand, the distribution of natural resources, upon which all extractive and manufacturing industries are based, is much more even. In fact, many important resources are most abundant in the lower-income countries. Thus the stage should now be set for a mutually beneficial global bargain.

However, the urge to reduce costs and maximize returns, coupled with the skewed concentration of capital, tends to force the costs of raw materials down and the prices of manufactured goods up. As a result, the global economy is lopsided, with a major share of returns going to a small proportion of the global population, mostly in the industrialized countries.

Changing the pattern

The environmental performance of industry and commerce is improving, but must improve more quickly. This imperative applies in all countries. Lower-income countries have to expand their industry to escape from acute poverty and achieve sustainability. In doing so, however, they must follow different pattern from that which has already blighted the environment in many areas of upper-income countries and on a smaller scale in many lower-income countries. Such development depends on the actions of industry, governments and the spread of technology.

The environmental performance of industry and commerce is improving, but must improve more quickly

The responsibility for clean industrialization falls largely on business. New technology is needed to clean up past mistakes and avoid future ones. It will be invented mostly by industry. Industrial development will need financing, and that will come largely from business and commerce.

A major share of the burden must also fall on governments, as regulators and managers of economic policy, and on environmental experts as the people who know most about the carrying capacity and resilience of the Earth. The process will involve consumers too, who can exert strong influence on companies through their buying power.

Many new technologies and processes will be perfected in the higher-income countries, and international help is needed to transfer them to the lower-income countries. Firms can become more involved by contributing personnel to help train overseas firms. Investment is needed to restore devastated environments such as those in Eastern Europe. Terms of trade will need to be reformed so that international markets may be opened for new products from the developing world.

Top left Drilling a core sample during a mineralogical investigation of Dumoga-Bone National Park, North Sulawesi, Indonesia. The economic pressures on lower-income countries from powerful international mining companies and international markets often make it very difficult for these countries to control the exploitation of their own resources or to protect their environments.

The tourism industry

Although it is not an extractive industry – it does not harvest nature – tourism uses and affects natural resources. To a large extent its viability depends on environmental quality, but its infrastructure of hotels, transport and other facilities and its influx of visitors can cause pollution, put pressure on resources and degrade ecosystems.

Experience shows that, to be sustainable, tourism has to be planned and regulated. It must be integrated with other land uses, especially in protected areas, and potentially damaging developments should not be permitted. Control should extend to the impact of tourism on people. Tourism's erosion of local cultures is hard to avoid. What is avoidable, however, is its occurring without people's consent, as happens all too often. Those affected by tourism must be involved in decisions on development and be able to modify or block what they see as inimical to their life style and environment.

On the other hand, tourism's importance as an industry should be recognized when decisions are taken about the use of national resources. At present, extraction industries tend to be given priority. Tourism's vital stake in natural and cultural heritage is often overlooked. Moreover, if managed correctly, tourism in protected areas may become a very effective instrument and source of finance for conservation.

Above On the beach in southern France. Much of the Mediterranean coastline is now a dedicated pleasure ground. Over the years, holiday beaches have become extensions of cities and the tourists find little left of nature.

Right So-called disposable packaging makes up much of the detritus that washes up on the coast of Greece after the annual tourist tide. Each piece of unsightly and often dangerous litter results from a thoughtless and avoidable human action.

Business sense

Businesses can make ethics for sustainable living a part of their corporate goal. This means adopting practices that build concern for the environment into business. It means introducing processes that minimize the use of raw materials and energy, reduce waste and prevent pollution. Toxic chemicals should be used only as a last resort and wastes minimized. Potentially harmful substances should be contained by management throughout the manufacturing cycle. Products should be environmentally friendly, with minimum impact on people and the Earth. The life of products can be increased and when they cease to be useful, industry should recover components and recycle materials.

Caring for the environment is good business

Many firms have recognized that caring for the environment is good business. This is not just a matter of public relations. Energy efficiency, waste reduction and pollution prevention can raise profits (see box opposite). Practices now limited to a few far-seeing companies will spread. The inclusion of Environmental Impact Assessment (see page 142) in the planning of company policy, the conduct of environmental audits, and environmental performance as a factor affecting senior executives' salaries are likely to be among these.

Controls and incentives

Industry favours self-regulation. This is desirable in principle, but the record of many sectors of industry needs to improve before public confidence can be assured. Hence legislation and government regulation remain crucial. The Polluter Pays Principle (see page 56) and the User Pays Principle (see page 39) can help shape policy.

Regulatory authorities could enforce standards for efficiency, waste disposal and pollution prevention. Standards for pollution should be calculated so that any permitted emissions will not harm human health or sensitive ecosystems. They should specify limits to the emission of hazardous substances which are as stringent as the best available technology can provide, and perhaps set even tighter standards, to enter into force at a specified date, so as to stimulate technological advance.

It is important that governments review existing economic incentives to industry, ensuring that measures such as taxes and subsidies promote conservation of energy, materials and water, and minimize pollution. They should remove incentives that conflict with these objectives.

Certain sectors of business demand special attention. Industries that use or produce hazardous substances should be persuaded to find safer alternatives. It is essential that they report any significant quantities of such substances held on their premises, and notify emergency services and the public what the risks are from them and what to do if there is an accident.

Top In Nairobi, Kenya, an improvised recycling plant turns old oil drums into a variety of useful containers and implements. Poverty is a strong incentive to avoid waste and make best use of resources. Most of the energy used in this recycling comes from human muscles.

Benefits of preventing pollution

A study of 500 industrial firms that took steps to reduce waste and prevent pollution shows that the benefits to companies can include:
• Lower expenditure on raw materials and energy
• Lower waste disposal costs
• Reduced future liability for the clean-up of, or contamination by, buried wastes
• Lower risks to employees and the public (and hence potential expenses)
• Reduced liability insurance costs
• Better employee morale and improved productivity and product quality.

In these 500 cases, wastes were reduced by 85 to 100 per cent. The payback periods ranged from three years to just one month. The methods used included both improved technologies and the use of less polluting materials. Some companies that developed new processes have gone on to patent them and sell or lease them to others.

Above Thick air pollution obscuring the sun above an industrial complex on the outskirts of Mombassa, Kenya. The development of industry is often seen as the easiest path to economic growth, and maximum benefit is assumed to come from low start-up costs and immediate high return. This perception often means that little attention is paid to pollution or the careful use of non-renewable resources because suitable measures can increase short-term costs. Well thought out regulations and incentives are needed to balance perceptions.

Top right Hides being treated at a managed wildlife range in Zimbabwe. Providing that wildlife products are harvested sustainably, with careful controls in place, they can be a useful resource for local industry and provide an important source of income for local people.

Meanwhile, it is up to governments to pass effective legislation on the labelling, packaging, marketing and disposal of hazardous substances, and to press for more rigorous international agreements on screening the 1-2,000 new chemical products added each year to the estimated 70-80,000 substances already on the market.

Industries based on natural resources, such as minerals, timber, fibre and foodstuffs, have a responsibility to maintain their resource base and reduce their impact on surrounding ecosystems. The minerals industry faces a particular challenge since its resource is non-renewable. Slowing extraction rates and conserving reserves for the future is difficult in a competitive market. To do so, the industry has to apply plans that serve long-term as well as short-term interests. In addition, the industry must improve standards of landscaping during extraction and take action to prevent pollution by dust and water. Bonds deposited by firms before extraction begins would guarantee higher standards of site restoration afterwards.

The biotechnology industry is a special case. It is new, rapidly growing and uses genetic material in novel ways, such as the development of genetically altered micro-organisms. An international agreement is needed to establish how biotechnology and its products should be screened for safety and environmental acceptability. Agreement is also needed on how to protect the interests of countries conserving the biodiversity that provides the raw materials of biotechnology.

Priority Actions

1

Promote dialogue between industry, government and the environmental movement

Improving the environmental performance of the industrial sector is the joint responsibility of business and government, but both need to draw upon the expertise of environmental organizations. Co-operation is needed in:
• Establishing the ecological context within which industry operates as a basis for suggesting changes in practices, processes and products
• Consulting with regional or local communities on the pattern of industrialization that best suits them
• Setting goals for new technical developments that will reduce pressure on the environment
• Formulating new regulations and economic instruments that will foster better environmental performance
• Establishing monitoring and environmental audit procedures.

2

Enforce high standards backed up by economic incentives

Governments should enforce national and, where appropriate, international environmental standards, laws, regulations and incentives (such as taxes and charges) concerning:
• The health and safety of workers
• Energy-, materials- and water-efficiency of practices, processes and products
• Integrated approaches to pollution prevention and control
• Control over the manufacture, marketing, use, transport and disposal of toxic substances.
Standards have to be high enough to minimize any risk to the environment, but businesses should be free to choose how they meet them, because this promotes efficiency and innovation. Encouraging work has already been done in setting such standards, and governments must continue to foster such initiatives.

3

Ensure natural resources are used economically

Industries based on the use of natural resources have a special responsibility to care for their resource base. The depletion of non-renewable resources such as minerals should be minimized by curbing wasteful use. Industries based on the products of forestry, agriculture and fisheries should:
• Monitor their impact on their resource and adjust harvests where necessary
• Work with governments and conservation groups to develop management guidelines for sustainable use of the resource
• Abandon methods of harvesting that are indiscriminate (such as drift nets), damaging to the resource or cruel (inhumane animal traps)
• Discuss with local communities, especially of indigenous peoples, how to prevent damage to their interests and traditional ways of life
• Give support, including financial backing, to international and national agreements and organizations that protect the resource base that they exploit, and promote further research into its sustainable use.

Above At a logging camp in the Amazon rainforest, a worker explains the logging process to a researcher who is working for a conservation project. After the researcher has made his report, project officers will be able to recommend methods of logging that will minimize environmental damage and improve the sustainability of the logging operations. Dialogue between industry and advisers is essential if industries are to improve their environmental performance.

Above right At an Environmental Education Centre in East Java, Indonesia, participants in a human resources training programme learn the principles of recycling. Recycling is an essential element in improving the use of resources.

4
Apply stringent safeguards to hazardous industries and hazardous substances

Governments, industry and citizens' groups should co-operate to identify a list of hazardous industries and establish strict procedures for their siting and operation. There should be:
• Insistence on state-of-the-art environmental protection procedures, ensuring that the action to take in an environmental emergency is widely known in the community
• Clear labelling of hazardous goods when they are being transported and sold, and legislation to control their marketing and disposal
• Co-operation between governments to prevent and prepare for industrial accidents that could have an impact across national frontiers
• International agreements on the screening, trade and disposal of hazardous substances
• New technology to minimize the production of hazardous wastes and research to find new and safer substitutes for toxic chemicals.

5
Commit businesses to sustainability and environmental excellence

Commitment to sustainability calls for businesses to:
• Develop and publish a corporate environmental policy, adopted by the company's board of directors
• Make one of the company's board responsible for environmental policy, and provide adequate professional support
• Prepare an action programme to define objectives for all personnel, with guidelines on how they should be met, and review its progress regularly with environmental and safety audits
• Make success in meeting health, safety and environmental targets an important factor in pay and promotion
• Introduce education and training programmes so that staff understand what is expected of them
• Invest in research and development so as to improve the company's ability to prevent pollution, reduce waste and facilitate recycling
• Wherever possible, market products that are non-polluting, durable, recyclable or reusable and not wastefully packaged
• Build public confidence through consultation over new developments and open disclosure of information
• Help customers use products in the safest and most efficient manner. Businesses in upper-income countries should help with technical assistance and technology transfer to lower-income countries, and transnational companies should ensure that uniformly high standards are maintained throughout their operations. Companies should help international trade associations and labour unions to develop and provide environmental training.

Human Settlements

Humans are a social species. Throughout known history people have lived together in groups, often linked by kinship. Over time, as populations have grown and concentrated in favourable locations, so people have congregated in larger settlements bound not so much by kinship as by a wider sense of community. Today, the most common form of settlement is the village – a cluster of dwellings that houses between 100 to 10,000 people, and is generally flanked by areas of cultivation and pasture. In India, for example, villages make up over 99 per cent of all settlements.

Below A reed-hut village of the Bisa people, Zambia. The Bisa live mainly by fishing in nearby Lake Bangweulu, and the treeless lakeside margins provide fertile soil for crops. The Bisa settlements make few demands on the local ecosystem. If the huts were abandoned, all trace of their presence would disappear within a few seasons.

By the end of the twentieth century, half of humanity will be urban

Right A Besingi village, in the buffer zone around Korup National Park, Cameroon. All settlements affect the environment over a much wider area than that occupied by the buildings. A buffer zone is an area in which the environmental impacts of settlements are contained so as to protect the park itself.

The greater part of the world's population lives in rural settlements, but the proportion living in large urban settlements has been rising fast, especially over the last 200 years. In towns and cities, the immediate link with the countryside and farming land is blurred, replaced by a focus on commerce and industry. The concentration of so many people, from 10,000 up to several million or more, partly undermines the sense of community, as familiarity gives way to anonymity. At the same time, however, it helps turn urban settlements into bustling centres of culture, education, employment and service provision. Greater opportunities in cities combined with job shortages in rural areas have therefore led increasing numbers of people to migrate to urban centres. Their influx, added to a natural increase in the numbers of people already living there, has made the world's city dwellers the fastest growing sector of the human population. UN projections claim that, by the end of the twentieth century, half of humanity will be urban.

Settlements as ecosystems

However large a settlement may be, and however remote it may seem from nature, every village, town and city is intimately related with and ultimately dependent on its wider environment. At the most basic level, it depends on it for resources and to dispose of wastes. By the same token, the inhabitants of a settlement depend on one another and on their community organizations to manage the flows of resources and wastes. A settlement and its hinterland can therefore be regarded as a web of interrelated processes of energy and materials exchange; in other words, as an ecosystem. Such a concept facilitates better understanding of settlement problems by highlighting energy and material flows and the interdependencies among people, resources and the environment.

The ecological character of settlements is most clearly recognizable in the simple, more or less self-sufficient, settlements of antiquity. For thousands of years, human settlements consisted of a few dwellings grouped around a common meeting place. In most cases, their location was determined by the availability of natural resources – fresh water and good soil for growing food. Since the fertility of the soil could become depleted through overuse they were often temporary sites.

As farming improved – producing food in surplus to immediate local requirements – and as transportation was developed, the way was paved for larger, permanent settlements. Though these were inhabited by people exercising an ever-increasing range of non-agricultural skills, they remained dependent on the surrounding land and the farmers who inhabited it for their daily food. Similarly, villages and small towns depended upon water being available within walking distance.

Communal dependence

As human populations slowly increased, towns and cities attracted an ever larger proportion of people, drawn by economic, social and intellectual opportunity. The larger cities became, the greater their dependence upon the surrounding environment and on their citizens' communal efforts. Rome in the third century, with some 800,000 inhabitants, had to draw water through a remarkable set of aqueducts from as far away as 70 kilometres (40 miles) and distribute it within the city by a network of conduits and pipes. Increasing food demands by urban populations turned ever more of the countryside over to intensive production. Goods were distributed to town folk at central markets. Growing industries demanded more raw materials and fuel, and the urban transport necessary to deliver them.

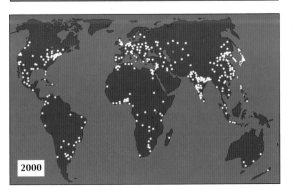

Above A magnificent view from the peak of Hong Kong island, which along with neighbouring Macau is the world's most densely crowded region. In Hong Kong, nearly 6,000 people are crammed into every square kilometre (16,000 per square mile). In Macau, the population density rises above 20,000 per square kilometre (52,000 per square mile).

Left Cities with more than one million inhabitants. Seen as if viewed from space, Earth in 1900 was illuminated by less than a dozen one-million-plus cities. By 1950, there were more than 50. By the year 2000, there will be at least 200 large cities on the face of the Earth, some with more than 20 million people.

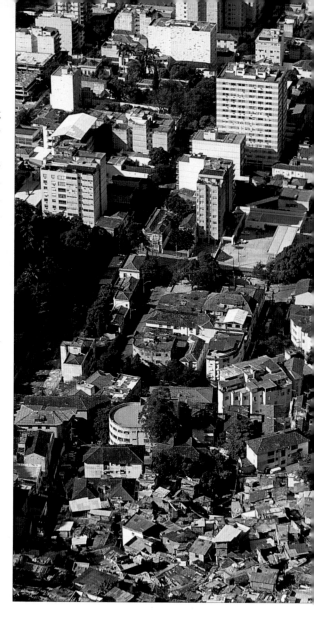

Below The growth of four cities in different parts of the world from 1950–2000. All four of them have undergone overall population increase, although New York, has also had periods of population contraction. New York's current annual rate of growth is only 0.16 per cent. By contrast, Mexico City has an annual rate of 4.3 per cent.

● Population in 2000

● Population in 1985

● Population in 1970

○ Population in 1950

New York
1950: 14.83 million
2000: 16.10 million

Shanghai
1950: 4.3 million
2000: 14.69 million

Tokyo
1950: 6.25 million
2000: 21.32 million

Mexico City
1950: 2.97million
2000: 24.44 million

At the same time, the settlements were generating waste from homes, factories and vehicles in concentrations that could not be dispersed on site. Deposited in landfill tips, or released into rivers and the atmosphere, they were discharged into an ever wider environment. Through pollution and the demand for resources, the environmental impact of settlements inevitably increased.

Today, although settlements may draw on many resources from far beyond their surroundings, their ecological relationships are no less real. Their citizens still need food, energy, raw materials, secure water supplies and clean air. In drawing them in, processing them and creating wastes they generate impacts that may affect the ability of ecosystems to maintain supplies.

Giant cities

Until the latter half of the twentieth century, rapid urban growth took place mainly in today's high-income countries. The largest cities quickly became very large indeed. Between 1810 and 1871, New York grew from 100,000 to over 1 million inhabitants. It has since grown more than tenfold again.

Over the last 50 years, however, surging population growth in lower-income countries has propelled many of them into urbanization at an even dizzier rate. Driven from overcrowded land and lured by urban opportunity, rural migrants, sometimes leaving their native countries, have poured into cities in Asia, Africa and Latin America. Through the 1970s, Mexico City grew by half a million people every year, Cairo by a quarter of a million. In 1950 Buenos Aires was the only city outside the high-income countries with over 4 million inhabitants, but by 1980 there were no fewer than 22 cities of this size.

> **Through the 1970s, Mexico City grew by half a million people every year**

In most high-income countries, the growth of existing cities is now slowing, but fresh areas of countryside are being urbanized instead. A similar pattern is emerging around many of the more dynamic cities of Asia and Latin America, as non-agricultural industries and service enterprises develop in rural areas. By contrast, many African cities are adopting characteristics of the countryside. Because of the scarcity of jobs and the inadequacy of incomes, more and more lower- and even middle-income groups are now growing part of their own food in or close to the city.

Urban crises

Cities generate and accumulate wealth and are the main centres for education, new jobs, innovation and culture. But their vitality is at risk. Many cities are crowded, congested and inadequately serviced. Their enormous requirements for water, energy, foodstuffs and raw materials are straining their infrastructures. They disgorge huge amounts of waste and pollution that contaminate the air, soil and water both within and far beyond their boundaries. Although good planning could prevent it, they sprawl over and sterilize cultivable land. In other words, many urban ecosystems degrade the resources and services on which they depend.

The anatomy of the city is fundamental to its functioning. Transport systems link the various quarters, and join city to city. Their smooth working is essential if goods are to be moved and people to travel efficiently. Unfortunately, virtually all major cities were laid out before motor vehicles became common, and their road systems are often inadequate for present needs. In fact, many cities are grinding to a halt because of urban congestion, while noise and pollution endanger health and erode the quality of life.

Hydrocarbons and nitrogen oxides, emitted by gasoline-powered cars, react in sunlight to create an acrid oxidant smog that is a hazard to human health and damages vegetation. Air pollution is particularly severe in cities because of their high traffic densities and low traffic speeds, and because exhaust gases become trapped between high buildings. Slow-moving urban vehicles also waste energy. Inter-city traffic, likewise, is imposing a massive burden on highways designed for far lighter loads than they must bear now.

Only a minority of cities have efficient, safe, clean and attractive public transport systems that people are prepared to use in preference to private vehicles. Installation of rapid-transit systems such as metros and tramways is difficult and costly.

Equally onerous is the task of providing city dwellings with basic utilities such as power, clean water and sewerage. New underground systems of piping are needed in many cities where old systems have deteriorated and leakages and contamination have become commonplace. In many cities of lower-income nations, thousands of inhabitants do not even have access to piped water. They take drinking water from wells, streams and rivers, often contaminated by uncontrolled discharges from factories and overflowing open sewers.

Despite being centres of industry and commerce, many cities display extremes of poverty. In high-income countries, as older industrial towns decline and inner-city districts decay, the less educated, the poor and the elderly find themselves trapped and sometimes homeless in places where services are disappearing and crime rates are high. Ethnic minorities, immigrants and the disabled generally suffer disproportionately, the victims of a growing equity gap.

In lower-income countries, the proportion of urban inhabitants suffering from poverty and environmental degradation is much greater. It is common for half or more of a city's population to live in overcrowded inner-city tenements or illegal settlements where people erect crude shelters from whatever materials are to hand. For most, water supply, sanitation, garbage collection and access to health care are grossly inadequate. The environments in which they live are among the most life-threatening in the world.

Above An aerial view of Rio de Janeiro, Brazil, where new slums (lower part of picture) lie next to middle-class areas. Comfortable high-rise apartment blocks now look out over a sea of shanty dwellings. Rapid and chaotic urbanization is altering the geography of many cities as new arrivals colonize all available open space.

Right Poverty in the heart of the inner-city slum district of Rio de Janeiro, Brazil, where most dwellings consist of little more than a wooden box without sanitation, running water or electricity. A short distance from the glamour of Rio's nightlife, countless thousands struggle for existence in insanitary and overcrowded conditions.

Sustainable cities

Cities, despite all their seemingly intractable problems, can provide high-quality living for all their inhabitants on a sustainable basis. The deprivation suffered by the minority of urban dwellers in richer nations and the majority in poorer nations can be drastically reduced. In both instances, more effective and representative local governments and more far-sighted national governments are essential ingredients in finding solutions.

Although rapid population growth has created demanding conditions, the problems of modern settlements are due largely to failures in management. Governments at all levels have proven unable to match the scale of urban growth with adequate planning and provision of services. The failures are not merely administrative: in many cases they reflect historical and political influences. Much urban growth has outstripped the capabilities of city authorities because national governments do not grant them enough power to raise revenues and manage their own affairs. Government structures remain centralized, but, because each city is unique, local involvement in its management and development decisions is essential. In lower-income countries many urban governments are not even elected, yet representative government is perhaps the only check against neglect of the needs of poorer citizens.

For sustainable urban development to occur, there must be new partnerships formed between local people, citizens' groups, businesses and governments. Development plans have to be equitable, practical, sensitive to local norms and cultures, and welcome to the people who are concerned. They should gear change to an ecosystems approach that safeguards services and resources and maintains a high-quality environment.

Managing for change

City authorities can do much to improve the pattern of urban growth by applying development control laws stringently and implementing plans that have been forged with the help of the local community. These plans must make sure that the city's expansion avoids prime farmland and wildlife habitat. They should set aside space for urban parks, squares and children's play areas. Plans could also encourage new sustainable activities that will create extra employment and income.

Above Rubbish dumped along the delta of the Lena River in Siberia. Even small human settlements produce large quantities of refuse and waste, which is often disposed of with little care for problems in the future.

Above right The evening rush hour in Buenos Aires, Argentina. Cars are widely regarded as a symbol of personal freedom and status. As a result, there is often considerable resistance to regulation of their use.

Right A vegetable stall run by a child in a village on Nosy-Be Island, Madagascar. Settlements are usually the focal point for organized or co-operative human activities, such as the exchange of goods and of information.

It is important that authorities charge all businesses the full price, through taxes and charges, of utilities and services, including the costs of their impact on the environment. This, along with full enforcement of laws and regulations, should help reduce urban pollution.

Positive actions in the perennial problem areas of housing, transport and waste have been tested by progressive administrations. For example, one way to alleviate housing shortages with relatively low expenditure by local government is self-help housing schemes giving people the chance of sites, materials and credit at affordable costs.

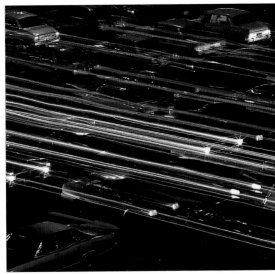

The mushrooming illegal settlements that ring the bigger cities of lower-income countries cannot be kept in check through eviction and demolition. The best long-term solution is to legalize the settlements and arrange fair compensation for the original landowners. The inhabitants need decent water supplies, sanitation, roads and community facilities. These can usually be provided through co-operative effort, using the organizing power of "barefoot architects" – local individuals with get-up-and-go. Gaining access to basic services often motivates people to improve their housing to regulation standards, and gives them a full sense of citizenry with all its rights and obligations.

Action to reduce congestion, pollution and energy wastage on city streets must include incentives for people to change from private to public transport. Bus and rail services need to be quick, frequent and pleasant. Concessionary fares are worth considering, especially for the elderly and lower-income groups. New technology also has a vital role to play. The use of energy-efficient, non-polluting vehicles should be promoted.

Plans should adopt an ecosystem approach that safeguards services and resources

Electric and hydrogen-powered vehicles could have their advantages if inexpensive, high energy-density batteries and improved methods for generating and storing hydrogen can be developed.

Modern electronic communication may soon make many journeys unnecessary – the movement of information rather than people is set to become more important. City authorities, national governments and industry should collaborate to make communication networks as efficient as possible.

Managing the mountainous waste output of urban areas in high-income nations becomes less difficult if government, community groups and businesses work together to reduce and recycle waste. Many citizens of lower-income countries are already extremely efficient at conserving resources. Every item of waste that has some value is reclaimed, either at source or by sifting through dumps. Such action is often driven by poverty, but in some cities, such as Shanghai, this reclamation is explicitly promoted by government policy. City authorities should foster such resource-conserving activities and the employment they generate, while improving the economic returns to the people and addressing the health risks involved.

Priority Actions

1

Adopt and implement an ecological approach to human settlements and planning

Communities need to adopt an ecological approach to ensure environmental concerns lie at the heart of the planning process. A strategy based on such an approach can be expected to:
• Improve and ensure water supplies
• Minimize the problems associated with waste disposal
• Reduce the diversion of high-quality land from agriculture
• Foster energy-conserving life styles and industrial practices.

2

Develop more effective and representative local governments, committed to caring for their environments

Local governments need to be able to:
• Provide essential services and utilities (especially health care, family planning services, emergency protection, safe and efficient public transport, traffic management, water supply, sewerage and solid waste disposal)
• Establish legislation, systems of regulation and local offices that meet citizen's needs for guidance and support
• Support neighbourhood centres run by citizens' groups to advise people on matters such as health care, self-help housing and efficient use of energy, water and materials.

3

Make the city clean, green and efficient

City administrations should make municipal energy use sustainable, and improve the quality of the air, water and urban amenities. They should ensure that local industry complies with standards and regulations. Specifically they should:
• Reclaim derelict land within their borders, using it for purposes such as housing, public open space, food production or industrial development
• Plan and create green space and green belts, including such things as community forests and woodlands
• Promote energy conservation, waste reduction and recycling
• Ensure that the city's waste collection and disposal services measure up to the highest standards
• Operate efficient waste water and sewage treatment processes, purifying the water for re-use and processing sewage sludge for fertilizer.

Left Raw sewage runs down the middle of the street in an area of illegal housing in Korangi Town, Karachi, Pakistan. Water pipes run through the sewage.

Below left Learning about conserving energy in cooking at the East Java Environmental Education Centre.

Right Children put glass bottles for recycling into bottle banks that have been provided by local government.

Below Heavy traffic in Karachi, Pakistan. Limiting private traffic can allow public transport to run well, encouraging its use and so decreasing pollution and congestion.

4

Develop an efficient and sustainable urban transport policy

To reduce congestion, pollution and use of energy in urban transport municipal and national authorities should:

• Encourage a switch to public transport by providing swift, safe, clean and efficient services based on people's needs

• Speed bus travel by providing segregated lanes, and help cyclists by giving them separate, safe routes

• Speed all road travel by establishing urban clearways on which parking is prohibited at peak periods

• Consider road pricing schemes and other devices that charge users of private vehicles the full social cost of their travel

• Establish pedestrian areas

• Avoid creating satellite cities and dormitory developments that increase the use of energy in transport

• Impose standards for fuel efficiency and pollution prevention

• Set targets for the improvement of technology, including the development of vehicles that do not burn fossil fuels and do not pollute.

Farms and Rangelands

Above A herder of the Peul people drives his goats along the shore of Lake Tabalak in Niger. Raising livestock is in many places a traditionally nomadic activity, as herds must move if land is not to be overgrazed. Goats are the hardiest and most agile of domesticated animals, and can extract nourishment where sheep or cattle would starve. In doing so, goats can easily overgraze the land and destroy all the vegetation.

Above right Rice paddies in Madagascar. Although rice is predominantly grown in China, India and South-East Asia, it has become important in other areas with a warm moist climate. Rice is a labour-intensive crop.

Far right Tea picking near Puncak, West Java, Indonesia. Tea is a high-value cash-crop grown on large commercial plantations. Although planting and growing is largely mechanized, harvesting is still done by hand and depends on cheap labour.

Although the origins of agriculture were before recorded history, we know that by about 9,000 years ago people on Earth had started to cultivate and tend some of the plants and animals they had previously only collected or hunted. So began the deliberate modification of ecosystems to increase the abundance of species useful to people for food or fibre. So also began the perhaps unknowing manipulation of species, the accentuation of their desirable qualities through selective breeding.

The cultivation of cereals (such as wheat, barley, millet, rice and maize), which are foods that can be safely stored for future use, enabled early farmers to enjoy the benefits of a relatively stable food supply. Probably at about the same time, the first animals were domesticated. Gradually, the variety of crops and livestock increased.

More people are hungry now than ever before, and their numbers are growing

Around 5,000 years ago, in south-west Asia, barley, wheat, flax, dates, apples, plums and grapes were being grown, and herds of sheep, goats, pigs and cattle were kept. By the same time, oxen and asses were pulling simple ploughs, sickles were being used for harvesting and wagons for carrying grain. Water supplied by irrigation canals was already enhancing cultivation on land otherwise too dry or unreliably watered.

Agricultural advances

For several thousand years farming techniques gradually spread, while agricultural tools and implements became easier to use and more efficient. With the period of world exploration in pursuit of trade, there was an increased exchange of many food plants between the continents. New World crops such as maize and potatoes became staples in the Old. Wheat and barley, cattle, sheep and chickens from the Old World became of great importance in many parts of the New.

The furthering of scientific enquiry in the modern era led to tremendous changes in agriculture. The invention and continual improvement of implements greatly reduced the time required for seeding, cultivating and harvesting, especially when machinery, powered first by steam and then by fossil fuels, was developed to run them. Artificial fertilizers and, later, chemical pesticides were formulated and applied to soils and crops. While these aids all reduced the labour input of agricultural production, they increased the input of energy. The increased yields per hectare that are

Shortages and land loss

Farming dominates the landscape across great stretches of the world. Yet in spite of the huge area of land now under cultivation, more people are hungry now than ever before, and their numbers are growing. Because too little food is produced where they live, or they are too poor to buy it, 950 million people in lower-income countries (excluding China) do not eat enough for an active working life. This is 19 per cent of the world's population (in 1980 the figure was 16 per cent).

Lack of food is most severe in sub-Saharan Africa and southern Asia. Output per person in the former has dropped at about 1 per cent a year since the early 1970s. The shortfall in production in these countries is closely linked to an increasing reliance on imported food, including food aid, and an emphasis on growing export crops. With grave consequences, especially for the future, it is also linked to the fearful scale of land degradation.

No less than 15 per cent of the Earth's total land surface is now affected by human-induced processes of soil degradation. Each year, an estimated 60-70,000 square kilometres (20-25,000 square miles) of agricultural land is made unproductive because of soil erosion.

thus achieved, combined with rising food imports, allowed food supply in the high-income countries to keep pace with a burgeoning non-agricultural population. Today, farming in such countries is essentially mechanized and with high energy input and demanding product standards.

In the lower-income countries, however, much farming remains at the artisanal level. Many farm units support their proprietors and families, and produce only a small surplus for local trade. In many cases, rising population is creating pressure for space on which to farm. A contrasting feature of such countries is industrial farming run by wealthy landowners and foreign companies, producing crops and livestock products for export.

Because labour costs are often low, mechanization is less advanced in low-income than in high-income countries, but fertilizers and pesticides are heavily used, often without adequate safety regulations. Many lower-income countries have vigorously promoted agricultural exports as a source of foreign exchange, with the result that their economies are dangerously dependent on them.

Waterlogging, and salinization and alkalinization (the accumulation of salts in the soil or encrusting its surface), generally caused by poorly managed irrigation schemes, reduce the productivity of an additional 15,000 square kilometres (6,000 square miles). On top of this, almost 10,000 square kilometres (4,000 square miles), much of it prime farmland, is lost each year to urbanization.

Land degradation is particularly widespread in vulnerable dryland regions, affecting almost 70 per cent of their area and leading to an estimated annual loss of production worth $42 billion. Much of the degradation is the result of unsustainable livestock farming, where the number of animals exceeds the carrying capacity of the grazing lands. There is understandable resistance to reducing herd sizes, but sustainability demands such action.

Intensive costs

In stark contrast, too much food is grown in much of Europe and North America, largely because of subsidies to farmers that increase production. The surpluses can be used as food aid to relieve shortages elsewhere, but this depresses markets for locally produced crops in lower-income countries and undermines their agricultural development.

Overproduction can be expensive both ecologically and economically. It claims land from natural habitats, reducing biological diversity as well as the attractiveness of rural landscapes. Intensive production favours monocultures (single, uniform crops), placing a strain on the nutrient supply and making them susceptible to disease. Partly in consequence, there is often heavy application of both artificial fertilizers and pesticides.

Increasing monoculture and the standardization of crops and livestock breeds across the world also threaten to reduce gene pools. Genetic variability within domestic species is essential for agricultural development, providing the raw material of plant and animal breeding. The adaptations of, and potential products from, traditional crops and wild strains of domesticated species that have fallen into disuse could also prove vital for future breeding and domestication. But many crops, threatened breeds and their wild relatives still await adequate conservation. Fewer than 30 per cent of countries, for example, have formal programmes to protect their plant genetic resources.

Other problems arise because the structure of world agriculture is changing. In high-income countries, family farms are being replaced by corporate holdings. In lower-income countries, programmes to increase production have concentrated where gains are likely to be easiest – on larger farms in relatively fertile and well-watered zones. In both cases, the lot of the small farmer and the rural landless is likely to worsen unless steps are taken to provide them with viable alternatives.

Promoting sustainable agriculture is essential in all countries. In the upper-income nations there is a particular need to remove marginal land from intensive cropping and to eliminate excessive subsidies. In lower-income countries, where increased food availability is paramount, priority should be given to increasing sustainable production on irrigated and well-watered land. The self-reliance of small farmers on marginal lands should also be improved and new techniques developed appropriate to local environments and economies.

Above At an agroforestry project at Talamanca, Costa Rica, project workers check on the growth of banana trees, which grow alongside other crops in a method of agriculture that minimizes environmental impact. The trees serve to protect the land beneath from erosion and to shelter the other crops, as well as providing a valuable harvest themselves.

Agroforestry

Agroforestry systems are methods of multi-crop production in which trees are an important feature. Generally speaking, the methods involve planting trees and various other crops in close proximity to each other. By providing both living cover and a mulch of fallen leaf litter, the trees protect vulnerable soils and young crops from damage caused by raindrop impact and by strong direct heat and light from the Sun. Some kinds of tree also increase the absorption of nitrogen from the atmosphere and so further enrich the soil.

Deep-rooted tree species help to reduce the loss of nutrients through leaching (washing away by water). The trees can also, of course, themselves provide valuable crops. The main forms of agroforestry include:
• Alley cropping, where annual crops are grown between lines of trees
• Mixed growth of permanent crops like coffee and cacao between timber trees
• Orchards, where the trees provide edible fruits, medicines and fuelwood, while the ground layer is cropped or grazed
• Plantations, where the ground layer of vegetation is grazed by livestock
• Shifting cultivation, where small, tilled plots are allowed to revert to forest after several years of cropping.

Land planning

The planning of land use must be an essential part of any national strategy for sustainability. In view of the scarcity of high-quality arable land and the rising demand for food and other agricultural products around the world, the land that is most suitable for crops should be reserved for agriculture. Urban developments or other developments that would take land out of agricultural use should be directed elsewhere.

In both high-income and low-income countries, however, there are significant areas of presently cultivated land and pasture that are not best suited to those uses. Perhaps because of steep slopes, thin soils or limited capacity to retain moisture they are not very productive or are particularly vulnerable to degradation. In high-income countries, many such marginal areas should be taken out of production. In lower-income countries, this is unlikely to be practicable as many people who lack other opportunities for employment live in these areas. The solution here is for people to adopt methods of farming with a lesser impact on the soil, especially those that are generally termed agroforestry (see box on this page).

Uncultivated ecosystems should be converted to agriculture only after careful assessment of the costs that would arise and the benefits that would result. Such conversion should not even be an option in countries with agricultural surpluses. Much land that is not now farmed has low agricultural potential because of such things as poor soil or low rainfall. The natural ecosystems on this land do, however, have value in maintaining life-support systems and biological diversity, and may also provide products such as timber, fuelwood, nuts, meat and other wild resources.

Far left Forest destroyed by slash and burn for agriculture, Kerinci district, Sumatra, Indonesia. Tropical forest can tolerate a limited amount of slash and burn farming, when it is practised by a small semi-nomadic population. However, with increased population pressure, slash and burn becomes the basis for permanent agriculture, and the forest and the fertility of the land are destroyed.

Below A deforested plateau in the Little Kaukasus region, Republic of Georgia. The natural tree cover of this upland region has been removed from any land suitable for arable or pastoral farming. Only the sides of river valleys, which are too steep for farming, are still wooded. Although the ecosystem looks superficially to be in good condition, erosion is already starting to form gullies on the slopes.

Improved husbandry

Farm land should be managed for improved, but sustainable, production through good husbandry. Soil and water must be conserved, and conditions for root growth improved. Good practices include crop rotation using plants that improve the structure and fertility of the soil, planting shelter belts to reduce wind damage, using small water retention structures, and providing a mulch of leaves, litter and crop residues to reduce raindrop impact, run-off and soil loss. Highly erosive lands may need a permanent cover of forage plants or trees.

In dry regions, land management can extend to water harvesting. This involves shaping farmland, through terracing and other methods, to slow the flow of water and so increase its infiltration into the soil. In low or unreliable rainfall areas, water harvesting can boost yields by 20–50 per cent, produce crops in years when they would fail without it and greatly reduce soil erosion.

Loss of organic matter through crop growth and leaching from the soil reduces the supply of nitrogen, decreases the soil's water-holding capacity and increases susceptibility to compaction and erosion. Consequently, replenishing organic matter is important in any farming system. There are many traditional ways of doing this, including the application of livestock manure, composting, rotational cropping using species that fix atmospheric nitrogen, concentrating livestock to graze fodder crops and enrich the land with their dung, multi-cropping and fallow periods. Such methods need to be maintained and improved.

Mixed farming systems, which traditionally integrate crop and livestock production, still have a key role to play in many regions. A central feature is the use of animal wastes as fertilizers. Separating livestock and crop production can turn animal wastes from a beneficial fertilizer into a costly pollutant. New ways to reintegrate crop and livestock production need development.

Some of the problems of agriculture can be eased by economic measures. In high-income regions especially, governments should end price supports and replace them with financial incentives for sustainable production, soil conservation and environmental improvement.

Land-use planning and good husbandry are essential parts of a strategy for sustainability

Above Terraced rice fields on the island of Bali, Indonesia. This is a traditional form of agriculture that can be highly successful. However, without constant attention to maintain the system of paddies and dykes, the soil would soon be eroded and washed away from the slopes by the rain.

Left Baskets of arrai fruit that have been gathered from the surrounding forest at a riverside market in Belem, Brazil. The harvesting and sale of such produce should be encouraged. Collecting the natural harvest of the forest makes far more sense that cutting it down to raise farm crops or livestock.

Chemical usage

Artificial fertilizers have an important, positive role to play. Countries with high populations relative to the area of good agricultural land have to achieve high yields to attain food self-sufficiency, and this generally demands the use of synthetic as well as organic fertilizers. Using fertilizers in drylands can double the yields of millet and maize and prevent the fertility of poor soils being depleted by overcropping. In much of Africa, however, because imported fertilizers are expensive they tend to be used only on commercial crops.

Fertilizers need to be made more affordable for many poorer farmers, but their use should still be cautious. In high-income countries, their use should be reduced. A tax on fertilizer use has been proposed for the European Community to reduce surplus production and encourage more sustainable use of land.

Pesticides, too, have been widely used to raise both crop yields and product quality. However, the excessive use of pesticides and fertilizers causes serious problems of soil, water and, in some cases, product contamination. Pesticides can be particularly harmful. In lower-income countries, an estimated 10,000 people die each year from pesticide poisoning, and about 400,000 suffer acutely. Certain pesticide residues travel long distances and build up in the food chain, affecting people and wildlife far from the places where they are applied. More than 500 species of insect and mite have developed a resistance to pesticides.

The application of pesticides must be controlled by effective regulations enforced by environmental protection agencies in all countries. Lower-income countries should remove or reduce subsidies on them to encourage their more careful use and to promote the adoption of integrated pest management (IPM), which is a broad approach to pest control that incorporates changes in cultivation techniques to lessen the impact of pests; increased use of pest-resistant varieties; encouraging the natural enemies of pests (by preserving their habitats); and careful use of chemical controls. In promoting IPM, Indonesia has saved $150 million a year by reducing its pesticide subsidy.

Priority Actions

1

Protect the best farmland for agriculture

Because high-quality arable land is scarce and the demand for food and other agricultural products is rising, land that is most suitable for crops should be reserved for agriculture as follows:
• Governments should map and monitor the extent of productive farmland and adopt policies that will prevent its loss to urban settlement
• Communities and local authorities should ensure these policies are implemented in their areas.

2

Improve soil and water conservation

Good husbandry is essential to prevent land degradation and improve conditions for crop production. Farmers should:
• Respect land capability; land should be used for the purposes to which it is suited
• Conserve soil; practices include improving organic content, soil structure and crop cover, the use of crop rotations and the proper use of fertilizers
• Manage rainwater; maintaining good levels of soil moisture is a key to soil conservation and enhanced production
• Reduce raindrop impact and run-off; doing so reduces selective removal of fertile soil, maintains infiltration and prevents the smoothing of soil surfaces
• Maintain plant cover; the more erosion-prone an area, the more urgent the need to establish dense and long-lasting cover
• Promote co-operation between technical staff and communities; locally developed schemes are far more likely to succeed than those based on top-down planning.

Below Dunes being stabilized with branches in Morocco. In many dryland regions, drifting sands and the degradation of formerly productive soils that can result from poor agricultural practices are severe problems.

3

Reduce the impact of agriculture on marginal lands

In both high-income and low-income countries there are significant areas of pasture and cultivated land that are not best suited to those uses. By and large, such areas should:
• In high-income countries, be taken out of production and restored to woodland and other natural ecosystems
• In low-income countries, be farmed under low-impact production methods, especially those methods that are generally known as agroforestry.

4

Encourage the adoption of integrated crop and livestock farming systems

Low-input, mixed farming systems generally involve the integration of crop and livestock production, and in some cases aquaculture. Animal wastes provide natural fertilizer for the crops and:
• Governments and farmers should work together to reintegrate crop and livestock production in ways most appropriate to particular areas, especially where artificial fertilizer is unavailable or too costly
• Small farmers, who have a wide and detailed knowledge of the local agricultural environment, should be consulted in setting research priorities and involved in testing new methods.

5

Increase the productivity and sustainability of dryland farming

To improve food supply and reduce the pressure to cultivate fragile marginal lands, rain fed (unirrigated) farming in dryland areas needs special management. It can be improved by:
• Soil and water conservation, including water harvesting
• Developing and distributing improved strains of staple crops that produce higher yields but retain drought resistance
• Using improved strains in traditional cropping systems, such as the combined cultivation of two or more crops with varying moisture requirements to insure against variable rainfall
• Increasing the use of fertilizers, particularly to correct nutrient deficiency.

Above right Local people collect manioc (cassava), a staple food, that has been left to soften in the Capim River, Amazonia, Brazil. Manioc can be grown sustainably in the forest. The plantations must be small and allowed to return to natural growth after very few seasons. Such agriculture can be combined with gathering natural rainforest products.

6

Promote the use of integrated pest management (IPM)

The aim of IPM is to keep pests below levels where they cause unacceptable damage, but to do so in an ecologically sound, as well as economically efficient, manner. Measures may include:
• Biological controls, encouraging the predators, parasites and pathogens that naturally attack pests
• Cultural controls, for example, cutting or uprooting noxious weeds, crop rotation, crop diversification, and timing of planting and harvesting to avoid peak pest periods
• Use of resistant or tolerant cultivated varieties of crop
• Release of sterilized male pest insects so that matings are infertile
• Chemical controls, such as pheromones (chemicals that attract insects) as well as minimal quantities of selective and non-persistent insecticides and herbicides.

7

Control the use of agrochemicals

A new balance needs to be struck in the use of fertilizers, pesticides and herbicides. Regulations and incentives can discourage excessive use and promote alternatives, and:
• Environmental protection agencies should enforce regulations concerning the allowable levels of pollutants in food and drinking water and the licensing, handling and application of pesticides
• High-income countries should consider taxing agrochemical inputs
• Lower-income countries should either remove or reduce subsidies for pesticides and herbicides

8

Conserve the genetic resources of agriculture

The gene pool represented by traditional crops and livestock is essential for the continuing development of improved strains and breeds and must be conserved. There is an urgent need to:
• Extend long-term protection to rare crops, unusual local strains of crop and their wild relatives
• Establish national plant genetic resources centres
• Establish a World Watch system on indigenous livestock breeds to identify when breeds are threatened and to promote action
• Strengthen the internationally supported Animal Genetic Resources Data Bank and complete the system of Regional Animal Gene Banks
• Support grassroots associations of farmers and gardeners for the maintenance of traditional and local strains and breeds.

9

Increase non-farm employment of small farmers and the rural landless

Attempting to provide alternative rural employment is a high priority in some countries, and:
• During slack agricultural periods, farmworkers could carry out public works essential for sustainable development such as reforestation, soil and water conservation works, installation of water pipes and construction of irrigation channels
• Alternative, permanent off-farm jobs should be created where there is too much demand for land. Rural industries can include such things as the processing of agricultural products and the manufacture of equipment for farming, forestry, water supply and construction.

10

Switch from price supports to conservation supports

Price supports in high-income countries help farmers avoid economic hardship, but cause excess production that furthers habitat loss and undermines the agricultural economies of lower-income countries. Governments could replace price supports with incentives to:
• Remove marginal land from agricultural production
• Protect uncultivated ecosystems
• Restore land productivity
• Adopt sustainable methods of land use and farming production.

Forests and Woodlands

Forest ecosystems cover 53 million square kilometres (20 million square miles) or 40 per cent of the Earth's land surface. They exist in an extraordinary variety of forms according to the climate, the soil, the lie of the land and the ways they have been used and modified by people. In some, trees are naturally spaced out forming open woodland or savannah; in others the trees crowd densely to create a closed canopy over the ground. Closed forests now cover approximately 29 million square kilometres (10 million square miles), four-fifths of their extent 300 years ago. Most of the cultivated and inhabited land of today was once clothed in forest.

The world's largest stock of trees lies in the great northern forest belt of Eurasia and North America, the taiga. The taiga, or boreal forest, is a relatively simple, species-poor ecosystem, dominated by conifers that can survive long, cold winters.

The temperate forests to the south of the taiga contain a greater variety of plants and animals, in various associations, including coniferous, broadleaf and mixed forests and the mixed shrublands that are characteristic of Mediterranean regions. Much of the area that they formerly covered has long been cleared for human occupation, and is now devoted to settlements, crops and pastures, with only patches of woodland remaining, and even fewer areas of old-growth forest. Temperate forests also grow in areas that have similar climates in the southern hemisphere.

Left Natural dry deciduous forest within the Huay Kha Kaeng Wildlife Sanctuary, Thailand. As well as providing refuges for animals, wildlife sanctuaries often preserve rare plants and habitats. Much of the world's dry forest has been modified or cleared completely.

Old-growth and modified forests

Throughout this chapter, "old-growth" forest means a forest in which trees have never been cut down or that has not been seriously disturbed for several hundred years. Equivalent terms are "natural" or "primary" forest. "Modified" forests are those in which trees have been felled during the past 250 years, usually by loggers or shifting cultivators, or from which other products have been harvested, but where there is a cover of indigenous trees and shrubs. The term modified forest covers many conditions, from light to heavy modification, and includes such areas as managed forests, where a deliberate effort is made to enhance or sustain the yield of products from the forest, particularly timber.

Above A remnant of old-growth tropical rainforest on Sumba, an island province of Indonesia. Massive deforestation during the last 100 years has in many places reduced the natural forest cover to a few isolated areas that are encircled by extensively modified land.

Left Natural deciduous woodland in Dartmoor National Park, England. Although this forest has existed in close proximity to human settlements for over 4,000 years, it has not been modified to any great extent, and retains much of its original character. The forest's survival is probably due to its position on a boulder-strewn slope.

Forests are highly diverse ecosystems, supplying many resources and generating vital income and employment. The annual value of world production of lumber, veneer, pulpwood and fuelwood exceeds $300 billion. Fuelwood contributes 19 per cent of the energy supply of lower-income countries. Forests also yield large amounts of forage, food, medicines, non-wood fibres, furs and skins, gums, waxes, latexes, resins, and other non-timber commodities. The economic value of these products, harvested sustainably, may exceed that of the timber removed by unsustainable logging.

Forest genetic resources include those used to improve the performance of trees grown for timber, wild relatives of crops and livestock used by plant and animal breeders, and species with potential as new products. Forests are important for tourism and are of inestimable cultural value.

Deforestation pressure

Some conversion of forests to agriculture and other land uses is inevitable, given the continuing increase in human population, but extensive tracts of forest are essential for life and human welfare. If managed sustainably it is possible for them to meet the large, diverse and often conflicting demands that people make on them.

Now, however, forests are being destroyed or degraded almost everywhere, causing not just the loss of natural ecosystems, biodiversity and renewable resources, but also serious problems of soil erosion, siltation and flooding. Some regions experience unreliable rainfall after deforestation, and large-scale deforestation in the tropics is perceived as a major contributor to global warming.

Boreal and temperate forests are no longer declining in total extent – in some parts of Europe and North America, forests are expanding across abandoned farming land – but they are subject to major changes in richness and distribution. One such change is the continuing depletion of old-growth forests. The temperate forests in the northern hemisphere have been heavily modified for centuries and few natural stands remain. In addition, modified forests have been degraded by unsustainable logging and fragmentation as a result of urban growth.

Logging in many northern forests has already taken place several times and can produce reliable yields of timber. This is especially so with selective harvesting of individual trees and small clearcuts (felling in blocks) of species that grow quickly. There is some doubt about the sustainability of large clearcuts, particularly in boreal forests or in those temperate forests with a predominance of slow-growing species.

Tropical forest ecosystems, particularly the rain forests, are the most species-rich of all. Forming an evergreen girdle on the land around the Equator, they support not only an immense variety of trees and other plants, but also abundant animal life. Much of the variety of animal species occurs at the upper levels, of the dense forest canopy.

In less well-watered areas of the tropics there are dry forests, less dense and luxurious, but characterized by thicker undergrowth. The savannahs, where scattered trees and shrubs are interspersed with patches of grass and herbaceous plants, are home to large herds of grazing mammals and their predators. Three quarters of the world's open forest and shrubland are in the tropics (mostly in Africa), along with 42 per cent of closed forest.

Natural and modified forests provide human beings with a wealth of benefits. Forests are an integral part of the Earth's life-support systems; among other things, they are major stores of carbon. In absorbing and releasing heat and water, they play a crucial role in regulating climate.

Locally, forests tend to temper climates, providing generally milder, moister and less variable conditions than places without forests in the same region. They also regulate the movement of water, protecting soils from excessive erosion, reducing the silt loads of rivers, and moderating floods and other harmful fluctuations in the flow of water.

Almost 15 per cent of the standing timber of 17 European countries has been moderately to severely damaged by air pollution. This takes two forms: acid rain derived from sulphur and nitrogen oxides, and oxidants produced by chemical reactions involving motor vehicle emissions (see Air and Atmosphere, page 118). It has been estimated that the productivity of European forests is declining at $30 billion a year. Acid rain and oxidants are also damaging forests in eastern North America, and are likely to do so in areas such as north-east China unless industries adopt modern pollution prevention technology.

Tropical forest loss

Every year, at least 180,000 square kilometres (70,000 square miles) of tropical forests and woodlands are cleared for farming, settlement and development projects such as mines, plantations and industry. In addition, in dry regions, fuelwood cutting is seriously depleting forest resources. In Latin America, the chief causes of deforestation are cattle ranching, land speculation, unplanned settlement in the wake of road building and unsustainable shifting cultivation – where cleared areas are not left to lie fallow for long enough or at all. These destructive changes have been favoured by policies intended to promote economic growth and land colonization. In Africa and Asia, the main causes are shifting agriculture, conversion to commercial agriculture and fuelwood cutting.

Every year, at least 180,000 square kilometres of tropical forests are cleared

Another 44,000 square kilometres (17,000 square miles) of tropical moist forests are logged each year and then left to regenerate. Logging is seldom a direct cause of forest loss, but its incidental effects can be great, both because of its immediate disruptive effects on the habitat and because logging roads allow settlers to penetrate and establish permanent clearings. Even selective logging tends to degrade the forest, sometimes heavily. Felling and removing of trees damages neighbouring seedlings and unharvested trees. It accelerates erosion through the clearance of land for roads and timber yarding areas, and logging on steep slopes. It creates fire risks by opening up the canopy, allowing the proliferation of easily-combustible herbaceous vegetation and the drying of logging debris. All these problems are made worse by recutting before there has been adequate recovery.

Top A Masai woman in Tanzania carrying a day's supply of firewood back to her family. Either burned in its natural state or converted to charcoal, fuelwood is a major domestic energy source, particularly in lower-income countries in dry regions of the world.

Above Cattle roaming on rainforest land that has been deliberately cleared by fire in Amazonia, Brazil. Many of the cattle that are raised on former rainforest land are destined for export to meet the demand in higher-income countries for supplies of cheap meat.

Right Road grading west of the Matto Grosso, Brazil. Road construction is often the first step towards large-scale rainforest clearance, giving access to both commercial interests and migrant farmers. Forest around the road is quickly destroyed and side roads develop.

Careful logging management could go a long way to avoiding many of these problems, but by 1989 only 10,000 square kilometres (4,000 square miles) of tropical forest were demonstrably managed sustainably. This represents a tiny fraction of total logging. At least 450,000 square kilometres (175,000 square miles) of sustainably managed forest would be needed to supply the current annual volume of the international tropical timber trade alone. The current domestic timber needs of producer countries would require nearly four times as much again.

Several factors underlie the destruction of tropical forests. One is inequitable distribution of land and economic power, which enables the wealthy to liquidate forests for profit, and forces large numbers of the landless and near-landless into forests to clear them and try to farm land that is unsuitable for agriculture. Other factors include insecure land tenure for forest dwellers, which leads to short-term maximization of profits and inefficient use of existing farmland elsewhere because there is no motive to farm sustainably. All of this is exacerbated by high rates of population growth and increasing demand for the products of tropical forests in high-income countries.

Forest policy

The world's forest estate needs to be valued as a priceless resource, to be sustained for the long-term benefit of humanity. Some of the actions that would help protect it, including curbs on air pollution and safeguards for biodiversity, are part of the wider process of conservation. But others are specific to the ways societies use and manage forests.

Good decisions on forest resources must be based on sound forest policy. However, most forest policies are aimed primarily at timber management. The interests of communities and the many sectors that use or influence forests, from tourism to water supply, are seldom paid adequate attention. The single-sector approach, with separate policies for agriculture, industry, settlements, energy and finance, rarely recognizes the impacts of these sectors on forests.

Nowhere is the need for greater integration of policies more pressing than in tropical forest regions where small farmers need assistance to give up unsustainable shifting cultivation. Land reform combined with policies to promote agroforestry and other sustainable techniques would help, as would stimulating alternative employment, including full processing of forest products.

Right Taiga with many lakes in the Mackenzie Lowland, Canada. The northern forests provide a large amount of the world's commercial timber. Although extensive, such forest needs protection from unsustainable logging.

Far right Tapping rubber near Rio Branco, Amazonia, Brazil. Controlled tapping of wild trees does not harm the forest. However, plantation monocultures – such as rubber or coffee – require destruction of natural forest.

Below Brazil-nut trees stand in isolation, Amazonia, Brazil. Because of their commercial value, the trees are protected by law. However, without the rainforest that once surrounded them, the trees do not produce nuts.

Space for forests

To ensure that sufficient land remains forested, each country should prepare a land-use strategy, based on broad consultation, that sets national targets for the amount of land to be kept under old-growth and modified forest. The area reserved will vary according to the natural conditions, area and existing settlement patterns of each country, but , with some obvious exceptions, not less than 10 per cent of total land area should be maintained under old-growth, some of it in totally-protected areas.

Some modified forest can be allocated for utilization, so long as it is sustainable. This could range from very light harvests of a few non-timber products to more intensive management designed to enhance long-term yields of timber. In Brazil, for example, extractive reserves, where activities such as rubber-tapping and the harvesting of fruit and nuts are allowed, have been established. Laos aims to earn 50 per cent of its forest revenues from non-wood products by the year 2000.

In some regions, especially the Amazon Basin, forest areas are of such global importance for bio-diversity and to the environment that as much as possible of the remaining forest should be maintained in an old-growth or lightly modified state.

Tree planting and reforestation is no substitute for the conservation of old-growth forests, but if it is well managed and has local support it can be of considerable benefit as a natural habitat and amenity. Plantations can take pressure off natural forests by producing large volumes of timber fast. Short-rotation fuelwood plantations are urgently needed in many tropical countries. Long-rotation plantations, which have time to build up richer stores of carbon, could have a major role to play in moderating climate change.

Global co-operation

International co-operation on forest conservation has already started. The two biggest initiatives in this area have been the Tropical Forestry Action Plan (TFAP – see box below) and the International Tropical Timber Agreement (ITTA). The ITTA calls upon its signatory nations to develop policies on sustainable use and conservation of their forests. However, another international accord, the General Agreement on Trade and Tariffs (GATT), counters this by preventing countries using trade tariffs, quotas or bans to favour trade in sustainably produced timber. The GATT, it has been proposed, should be amended accordingly.

An international forest convention has also been proposed. This could enhance co-operation by promoting: clear criteria on which sustainability can be assessed; trade measures to encourage sustainability; compensation payments to low-income countries in exchange for conservation measures of global significance; and funding to conserve forests especially important for biodiversity. The convention could also sponsor a wider range of programmes than at present, including a Temperate Forestry Action Programme to improve temperate and boreal forest management.

Timber trade

Much needs to be done to make the logging industry more sustainable, especially in tropical countries. Sustainable practices may yield less profit in the short term, but if present practices continue the industry's long-term future. will be jeopardized Better management of logging may include: limiting cutting to a level from which natural regrowth can rapidly make up the deficit; selective felling of commercial trees to avoid the wastage of clear-felling; strip-felling along contours to avoid excess run-off and soil erosion; well-managed re-planting; and avoidance of damage to unharvested vegetation when felling and transporting logs.

Consumer action can be important in encouraging sustainability. Consumers should be willing to pay more for certified products of sustainable management and avoid those produced unsustainably. Blanket boycotts on tropical hardwoods are, however, counter-productive. They penalize products that have been produced sustainably, and may favour forest clearance because they remove the economic incentive to keep even modified forests.

Consumers can also reduce the pressure on forests by using wood more efficiently, demanding recycled products and recycling what they buy. At present, for example, large amounts of wood are wasted in most construction and demolition sites in high-income countries.

The Tropical Forestry Action Plan

The Tropical Forestry Action Plan (TFAP) is a programme that has been set up by international development agencies with the support of national governments. It was launched in 1987 and aims to halt deforestation and increase the sustainable benefits from tropical forests by: improving the lives of rural people; increasing food production; stabilizing shifting cultivation; ensuring the sustainable use of forests; conserving forest ecosystems; increasing supplies of fuelwood; and expanding employment opportunities for people who live in forest regions.

Although it has doubled the amount spent on tropical forests, the TFAP has not achieved what it set out to do, because of shortcomings both in its organization and its priorities. A common criticism is that it fails to address the link between large-scale development projects and deforestation. Recommended improvements to the TFAP include: making its planning bodies fully independent; ensuring technical advice comes not just from foresters but also from experts in such areas as land tenure, community development, farming and conservation; and ensuring the involvement of local communities and special interest groups.

Priority Actions

1
Establish a comprehensive system of protected natural forests

Preserving forests in systems of protected areas should be a key element of land-use planning. Such systems should:
• Represent all national forest types
• Have as much variation as possible to guard against climate change.
A reasonable target for many countries is at least 10 per cent of land under old-growth forest. Protected areas should:
• Place a high priority on preserving old-growth forest ecosystems
• Be surrounded by large buffer zones of modified, managed or planted forest.

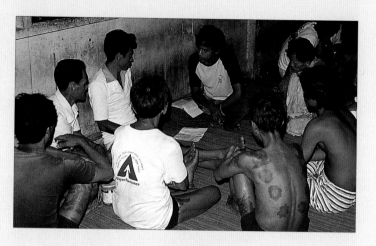

2
Maintain an adequate permanent estate of modified forest

Modified forests should be maintained to conserve life-support systems and biodiversity, while providing sustainable yields of timber and non-timber products. Sustainable use would be helped by:
• Giving communities a much stronger say in forest management
• Assigning timber-bearing land to the private sector on condition that all harvesting is sustainable
• Making land tenure conditional upon retaining a significant proportion of the land under forest cover
• Providing incentives for the private sector and local communities to develop industries that are compatible with multiple-use forestry, and for them to refrain from overharvesting
• Encouraging shifting cultivators, where possible, to farm in ways that will allow them to settle on permanent plots.

3
Increase the area of planted forest

Planting trees is important both for environmental improvement and as a way of relieving harvesting pressure on modified forests. Plantations can be an effective use for degraded lands and land that is to be retired from agriculture. Important planting schemes include:
• Reforestation of high ground to protect water supplies and reduce soil erosion
• Short-rotation plantations to produce sustainable yields of fuelwood
• Long-rotation plantations to provide timber for long-lasting products and to act as carbon-sinks to help moderate global warming
• Establishing trees in towns and along roadsides for amenity, to improve local climate and to reduce some air pollutants.

4
Increase capacity to manage forests sustainably

The unsustainable industrial exploitation of any forest, and of tropical forests in particular, must not go on. The following will help all countries achieve sustainable forest management:
• Establishment of a legally guaranteed permanent forest estate
• Provision of training in forest ecology and management
• Logging standards that define the amount to be cut, cutting cycles and acceptable harvesting techniques
• Adequate control over harvesting and replanting to ensure regeneration and minimize environmental damage
• Economic and financial policies that demand no more from the forest than it can yield sustainably
• Environmental policies that protect ecological services, biodiversity and the resource base of all forest users.

5

Strengthen community management of forests

Because they live with the forest, local people often have a strong incentive to use it sustainably. But this incentive is stifled if they are denied a fair share of the forest's resources, or if they feel powerless to influence key decisions made by corporations, wealthy individuals or government officials. To prevent this:
• Local communities that rely on the multiple benefits of forests should be involved in decisions on forest management and land clearance
• A larger share of management control should be returned to local institutions
• Central government should pass some of the tax revenues from forest industries on to local communities to strengthen interest in maintaining the resource
• Indigenous and traditional forest dwellers should have full and informed consent over forest operations.

6

Create a market for forest products from sustainably managed sources

Rising demand for sustainably produced forest products provides a strong economic incentive for forest conservation. A healthy market for such goods depends on:
• Consumers seeking out products known to have been produced sustainably, and selectively rejecting those that resulted from forest clearance (such as beef from forest ranches) or that affected rare species, protected lands or the lands of indigenous peoples
• Industries and traders establishing labelling and tracking mechanisms to allow consumers to assess the sustainability of production processes, especially those involving tropical hardwoods and veneers.

7

Set logging taxes and charges to reflect full social cost

In many countries, timber royalties and other charges for extracting wood are below true economic value and do not cover the costs of forest management and regeneration. This encourages wasteful exploitation. Governments should:
• Auction logging concessions to companies with high minimum prices to guard against bid-rigging
• Set licence fees high enough to discourage logging in stands of marginal commercial value, which are best left to grow undisturbed
• Charge extraction fees that reflect the full value of different timber species
• Abolish tax deductions and credit subsidies to companies unless their practices favour sustainable use of forests
• Raise export taxes on logs to favour domestic wood-processing, and hence increase the value added to exports and take some of the pressure off national forest resources.

8

Increase international co-operation

The international community can act to further forest conservation, particularly by helping lower-income countries maintain their forests. Lower-income countries also need favourable terms of trade for sustainably-produced forest products. Important actions include:
• Improving the TFAP to make it more independent of governments and industry and more responsive to social and environmental objectives
• Amending the GATT to enable countries to use import restrictions to discriminate between sustainably and unsustainably produced timber
• Developing an international forest convention to deal directly with forest conservation and development and help harmonize ecological and economic approaches to forest resources.

Top left A forest guard discusses proposals for a wildlife sanctuary with representatives of the Iban people in Malaysia. To achieve success, sanctuaries and reserves need to have the willing co-operation of local indigenous populations.

Left Planting out pot-raised seedlings at a tree nursery in the Udzungwa Mountains, Tanzania. This is one of many such projects funded by international conservation groups. Many more projects are urgently needed.

Above A farmer prepares land by slash-and-burn methods in the Kerinci area of Sumatra, Indonesia. Because of rapidly expanding population, this area is currently losing 3 per cent of its forest annually.

Fresh Water Systems

Life on Earth depends on water. Our planet is the only one where water is known to exist in liquid form. Water is a unique solvent that carries the nutrients essential for life. How people use the land and change ecosystems affects the quality, movement and distribution of water. In turn, how people use water affects the integrity of both land and aquatic ecosystems.

The fresh water vital to human existence forms part of a great global cycle. There is an unending movement of water falling from the sky as rain or snow, seeping through the soil and into permeable rock to form ground water, flowing across the landscape through streams, rivers, lakes and wetlands, spilling into oceans and rising – through evaporation – back into the sky.

Fresh water is absorbed by plants and soil dwelling animals. Other animals, including people, consume water by drinking and ingesting it in their food. The water that is found in plants, animals or in the soil is sometimes called "green water" to distinguish it from the "blue water" in rivers and other water bodies.

During its time on land, water flows downhill to gather in streams and rivers, which together form drainage systems. The total portion of land served by a drainage system is known as a drainage basin. The perimeter of higher terrain – for example, a range of hills – that bounds each drainage basin and separates it from neighbouring basins is termed a watershed.

As it cycles through its various stages, the movement of water is naturally regulated. Soil, vegetation, marshes and lakes impede downstream flow, act as temporary stores and partially even out fluctuations in river discharges lower down in the drainage basin. Forests in drainage basins with high rainfall are especially important, retaining water after rainfall and then steadily releasing it.

The total amount of water on and in the Earth and in the atmosphere does not change, although it may transform from liquid to ice or vapour, and may be temporarily lodged in living cells or locked up in chemical compounds. But in some places and at some times water may be the limiting factor for life. A water shortage is not so much a lack of supply as an imbalance between supply and demand.

Above Local river traffic near Maroancetra, northern Madagascar. In rural areas, natural waterways can be the only effective means of transport. River systems not only give easy access to the coast, they also provide local distribution networks.

Left A Piro Indian with a freshly caught catfish in the Manu Reserve, eastern Peru. For many in inland areas, freshwater fish are the only regular source of protein. Overfishing and pollution have led to widespread depletion of stocks.

Left In the water cycle (or hydrological cycle), water circulates from the oceans to land and back again. Water evaporates from the oceans (1), and some precipitates (in the forms of rain, snow, fog or dew) and falls back to the ocean (2). Water vapour is carried over land by winds (3), often forming clouds. Further water evaporates from land, some from rivers (4) and lakes (5), some from the soil (6) and some from plants (7). The water vapour may then precipitate over land (8), often over high ground. Some of the precipitation is quickly absorbed by vegetation (9), and some remains on or near the surface and runs into streams and rivers (10), flowing finally to the ocean (11). Other water enters the ground (12) to lie in porous rock (13), but above any impermeable layer of rock, where it is known as groundwater. Some of the groundwater enters lakes (14), and water in lakes may enter the ground (15). Other groundwater reaches the soil (16) and some makes its way directly back to the oceans (17). Problems of disruption and pollution may occur at all stages in the cycle.

Such an imbalance may occur because of a decrease in the supply of water available at a certain place and time, perhaps because of a decline in precipitation. It might be that heavy deforestation around watersheds has accelerated rainfall run-off, making river flow erratic. Often, however, shortages arise from a growth in demand, because of an increase either in the number of consumers or in the per capita rate of water use.

From the human point of view, there can, of course, be too much water as well as too little, leading to flooding. Naturally occurring fluctuations in stream flow can cause rivers to overflow – indeed, inundation of flood plains and deltas is important in renewing the high fertility of their soils. Abnormal floods, however, can damage crops, dwellings and roads, and threaten lives. Such events may be dangerously amplified by the removal of vegetation from drainage basins and by the draining and dyking of tributary wetlands that accommodate periodic surges of water.

Consumption and usage

The primary human need for fresh water is for drinking. However, this represents a tiny part of our water usage. Much more is used for cooking, washing and the disposal of wastes. Because water is a vital requirement for plants and animals, great amounts are also used in agriculture. Crop irrigation is the main consumer of water in most countries, accounting for about 70 per cent of world water withdrawals. The irrigated land area has almost tripled since 1950, and currently supplies one third of the world's food.

Fresh water is an essential element in many industrial processes. Lakes and rivers provide highways for the transportation of people and goods. Many are popular tourism and recreation sites.

Global water use has grown three to four times faster than the rise in population

They harbour fish and other useful animals and plants on which many people depend. To facilitate some of these uses, rivers and other water bodies have long been managed artificially by straightening and dredging, diverting and damming. Large dams are built to generate hydroelectricity and to secure water for irrigation and domestic supply. Such engineering has been a source of national pride and political prestige.

Above A desert well at Chami in the Banc d'Arguin National Park, Mauritania. Traditional materials and modern concrete have been combined to provide an accessible supply of drinking and irrigation water. The shallow trough next to the well is used for watering livestock. Desert nomads can be completely dependent upon the maintenance of such wells.

Global crisis

Our use of water is creating a crisis. Global water withdrawals are believed to have grown more than 35-fold in the past three centuries, three to four times faster than the rise in population. Current patterns of consumption cannot be sustained if the human population reaches 10 billion. Many countries already suffer serious shortages, yet water continues to be used wastefully. Less than 40 per cent of the water supplied for irrigation, for example, actually contributes to the growth of crops.

Misuses of water are having increasingly severe environmental impacts. Badly managed irrigation schemes have ruined large areas of formerly fertile soils through waterlogging and salinization. Unless action is taken, rapid increases in water withdrawals, particularly in semi-arid and coastal zones, will cause further salinization, poor water quality and, in some low-lying terrain, land subsidence.

> ## Misuses of water are having increasingly severe environmental impacts

As demands for water and energy have risen, major investments have been made in damming and diverting rivers. However, the benefits of large dams and other water engineering projects are usually not as large as foreseen, and their adverse effects have been gravely underestimated. These have included: disruption of river and coastal fisheries; erosion of river channels; flooding of natural ecosystems; displacement of inhabitants from reservoir sites; spread of waterborne diseases; and reduced total flow of water because of increased evaporation from reservoirs and irrigated lands.

Around the world, water quality is impaired, often severely, by pollution. Heavy metal pollution and contamination by organic pesticides and other toxic compounds is widespread and locally severe. Acidification of waters by sulphates and nitrates deposited as acid from air pollution is a major problem in Europe, North America and parts of Asia. Excess nutrients from waste water and fertilizer run-off cause algal blooms and deoxygenation of streams and lakes, damage fisheries, reduce biological diversity and render water unfit for drinking. Waterborne pathogens that thrive in conditions of poor water supply and inadequate sanitation are the biggest cause of death and illness in lower-income countries. Drinking and washing in such conditions bring the risk of infection with diseases such as typhoid, cholera and dysentery.

The productivity and diversity of freshwater ecosystems are further threatened by changes resulting from forest clearance, dams, channelling of streams and drainage of wetlands. Many fish stocks are also heavily exploited. Commercial fishing for distant markets threatens some otherwise sustainable artisanal fisheries.

The intentional and accidental introduction of exotic species of fish into freshwater ecosystems can devastate the native fauna. Any non-native stock used in aquaculture has a high chance of escaping into the wild, so suitable native species should always be considered first. Many aquatic plants are also causing problems.

Saving water

As population increases, the sustainability of water use ultimately depends on people adapting to the constraints of the water cycle. Human societies need to develop the ability – the awareness, knowledge, procedures and institutions – to manage their uses of land and water in an integrated manner. Ways need to be found to maintain the quality and quantity of water supplies, both for people and for the ecosystems that support them.

Reducing unnecessary demands on water supply is fundamental. To ensure supplies for public health and other essential uses, every consumer should use water more efficiently.

Top A banana plantation in Bocas del Toro, Panama. Banana plants cannot survive periods of waterlogging and thus extensive drainage is carried out. The drainage canals, apart from heavily modifying local ecosystems, carry the large quantities of fungicides, pesticides and fertilizers used on the plants directly into rivers.

Wetlands

Wetland ecosystems – flood plains, freshwater marshes, peatlands and estuaries – play a central role in the water cycle. They absorb flood waters and regulate floods, helping to ensure year-round water supply; they absorb nutrients and retain sediment, purifying water; they buffer wind and wave action, helping to protect coasts from storms. Many yield products that can be harvested sustainably, including fish, timber and crops. They also support important populations of wildlife and are a major recreational and tourist resource.

In the past, these multiple benefits were poorly recognized, and major development projects often sought to maximize use of only one resource. Many wetlands have been artificially drained. Up to 50 per cent of the wetlands that once existed have been destroyed or degraded.

The maintenance of water mains and the use of better technologies, such as micro-irrigation and waste-water recycling, merit special attention. Municipal waste water can be used to meet some irrigation needs, particularly in drylands. The chemical, pulp and paper, primary metals and food-processing industries should recycle the large quantities of water they use.

Media advertisements and awareness campaigns can help persuade people to reduce water consumption voluntarily. In drought conditions, prohibitions on non-essential uses, such as garden watering, automatic car washes and refilling swimming pools, are easy to police when public awareness of the need for water conservation is high. Such uses should generally be discouraged, perhaps by high charges, in arid and semi-arid zones of high-income countries.

Greater efficiency can result from economic incentives, such as charging the full price for water used. The full price reflects the costs of building and operating supply systems, of losses in distribution, and of protecting forests, wetlands and other ecosystems that regulate flow and maintain quality. Providing a reasonable supply of domestic water free of charge would prevent this measure harming the poor and disadvantaged in society.

For large segments of the world population, local rainfall is the only source of water. It is crucial that rains are used efficiently through careful land-use planning, water harvesting (for example, collecting rainfall), choice of crops and scheduling of crop planting so as to conserve surface and ground water for the most important uses.

Above Open latrines directly over a river in a slum district of Jakarta, Indonesia. It is not only the quantity of water available that is important but also its quality. Crowded conditions that have poor sanitation are excellent breeding grounds for water-borne disease.

Left A wetland landscape in the Haleji Lake wildlife sanctuary, Pakistan. Wetlands are some of the most frequently abused, polluted and destroyed ecosystems in the world. Those that remain relatively undisturbed are refuges for many endangered plant and animal species.

Bottom left At Kagungo in northwestern Nigeria, the traditional fishing festival celebrates the annual harvest of freshwater fish. Dried in the sun, these fish are a protein source that with proper management can last until the next annual harvest.

Integrated management

Integrated management of water and land uses would go a long way to solving many of the problems of water provision and quality, and of ecosystem conservation. Usually, however, the water cycle is divided into separate managerial parts: water management is considered separately from land management, ground water from surface water, and water supplies from aquatic ecosystems. One option is to place overall responsibility for co-ordination with the national environment agency. Another would be to establish a national land use authority.

The logical unit of water management is the drainage basin. All uses of water and land affect the quality and flow of water from headwaters to the coastal zone. Water policy within each basin should take account of – and balance – them all, and be based on an evaluation of the local capacity for water extraction and tolerance of pollution. Withdrawal from surface and ground water should not reduce river flow where this supports important ecosystems elsewhere in the basin. Pollution by non-degradable substances must not exceed levels that would endanger human health or ecosystem function. By the same token, biodegradable substances must not be released in such quantity that they exceed the capacity of ecosystems to break them down.

Given their importance in maintaining river flow and water quality, any degradation of watershed forests, forests around river systems and major wetlands is of concern. Large water management projects, especially dams, should only proceed when it can be shown that the project's

Integrated management of land and water uses would solve many problems

long-term benefits exceed the total costs of the scheme, including compensatory measures and damage to ecosystems.

Improved management will rely on improved information. Many regions lack instrument networks for measuring precipitation, river flow, evaporation and the quantity of ground water. Better information and advice also need to reach consumers, to persuade them that water is not limitless or free and that they should save water and protect it against pollution. In lower-income countries, campaigns are needed to reinforce the importance of improving hygiene and sanitation.

Community action

In many parts of the world, water and aquatic ecosystems have traditionally been managed as a community resource for drinking, irrigation, fisheries or fur harvesting. Such management has been weakened, in many cases, by increased population pressure on land and water, by excessive government intervention or (especially in open water fisheries) by the encroachment of powerful commercial interests. Good water management should draw on people's knowledge of land and water resources in their locality, and begin with sensitive participatory planning. It can then go on to establish a greater degree of community control.

Left The river port at Tefe, Amazonia, Brazil. The inhabitants of the surrounding "flooded forest" travel from remote regions by boat to obtain provisions. The river is at risk of degradation in various ways because of damage to the surrounding forests and pollution caused by increasing population.

Right Rebuilding homes after flooding near Bahawalpur in Pakistan. Despite the risks involved in living on river floodplains, the benefits of the fertility of such regions are great. Disturbing patterns of flooding through water-management schemes can damage this fertility.

Below Fishermen and egrets on the inner delta of the Niger River, Mali. This is one of the few permanently life-supporting regions in the frequently drought-stricken Sahel. Any proposals to manage the flow of this river must aim for minimal . environmental impact.

Community-level schemes, such as those that provide safe drinking water and improved sanitation, should be expanded. Among the successful programmes of this kind is the Hinduja Foundation's "Drinking Water for the Millions" in India. In many drought-prone areas of lower-income countries, returns to agriculture can be increased by community-based water harvesting and small-scale water storage projects.

Artisanal fishing communities are among the poorest groups in many societies. They are vulnerable to further impoverishment, because they often cannot protect their resource from fishing by outsiders or from habitat degradation. Such communities should be allowed to fish sustainably in protected areas. This would enable community members to pursue a traditional life style and, by giving the community an economic stake in the protected area and so motivation to care for it, could also improve conservation.

Shared problems

Some 40 per cent of the world's population lives in river basins shared by two or more nations. Yet more than one third of the 200 such basins are not covered by any international agreement, and fewer than 30 of them have co-operative arrangements to manage competing demands. Because pollution, impoundment and diversion of water by upstream nations look set to be rising sources of tension and insecurity, collaborative institutions such as the present Canada-United States International Joint Commission and the Mekong Committee are likely to grow in importance. Governments should also consider co-operative strategies such as the Rhine Action Plan to address priority problems.

Pollution and reduced flow also have major impacts on coastal waters. Because the water cycle includes fresh waters and oceans, the management of land and water uses should take account of the needs of management of ocean and coastal zones.

Restoring the benefits of fresh waters

Recognition of the value of freshwater ecosystems has, in many cases, prompted strong arguments for their maintenance and restoration. For example, successful preservation of 380 square kilometres (150 square miles) of wetlands in the valley of the Charles River in Massachusetts, United States, secured natural storage of seasonal flood waters. Had the land been reclaimed, the annual cost of flood damage would have averaged over $17 million. At the same time, valuable wildlife habitat has been saved.

Lake Fetzara in Algeria, drained originally by the former colonial administration, was reinstated in the early 1980s because it provided flood storage to protect the steelworks at nearby Annaba. This single purpose restoration has provided multiple benefits because the slow release of winter flood water is used for downstream irrigation, the re-established vegetation on the lake margins provides forage, and thousands of greylag geese have returned to overwinter at the lake as they did before it was drained.

In Denmark, in the 1960s, the delta of the Skjern River was pumped dry and dyked for agriculture. It is now being partially returned to marshes and a seasonally inundated floodplain. The aim is to reduce the pollution of the coast and sea by nutrients washed downriver. This will be accomplished partly by reducing the area of intensive agriculture and largely through the nutrient trapping capacity of the restored wetlands.

Priority Actions

1

Improve the information base

Sustainable management of water resources depends on adequate knowledge and research, directed towards complex tasks such as:
• Estimating and comparing the availability of water with national levels of water use and wastage
• Assessing possible changes in human population distribution and climate, and their likely impacts on water resources
• Monitoring water management activities, which would require assessing drainage basins and the total economic value of water resources, and considering the role of ecosystems in regulating water quality and flow, and in the productivity of fisheries and agriculture.

2

Increase awareness and training

Campaigns and education programmes can help persuade people to conserve and protect water and provide instruction on managing resources. Actions include:
• Creation of a basic understanding of the water cycle through teaching in schools, colleges and via the media
• Improving awareness of the values of aquatic ecosystems and the ways they can be used sustainably
• Explaining that everybody needs to protect water from pollution and giving advice on choosing less polluting household products
• Campaigning to improve sanitation, especially in lower-income countries
• Training programmes in the integrated management of water and aquatic ecosystems, both as courses in their own right and as part of courses in subjects such as engineering and economics.

3

Increase the efficiency of water use

Everyone should assign high priority to the more efficient use of water. Important considerations include:
• Better upkeep of water supply networks to avoid leakage
• Better upkeep and technology in irrigation systems to eliminate wastage
• Enhanced storage and conservation of surface and soil-water in areas where local rainfall is the only source of water
• Greater recycling of waste water
• Water conservation efforts in the home, such as repairs to dripping taps, and the installation of dual-flush toilets
• Continuing or seasonal limitations on non-essential uses, such as car washes and lawn watering.

4

Manage water and pollution on a drainage basin basis

Drainage basins are complex systems in which the effects of human activities are rapidly passed on to communities and ecosystems downstream. Water policy within each basin should reflect the following principles:
• Uses of water should be planned on the basis of their impacts on water quantity and quality
• Water allocated for domestic, industrial and agricultural consumption should be within the limits of sustainable supply
• Management of ground water extraction should minimize environmental damage such as salinization, land subsidence and reduced river flow; to maintain levels, the rate of pumping should not exceed the natural recharge rate of ground water
• Water quality standards should be established to protect both human health and ecosystems
• Potential health hazards, such as the spread of waterborne pathogens and malarial mosquitoes, should be considered when designing water schemes
• Potentially contaminating practices such as solid waste disposal in landfills and the use of agrochemicals should be carefully controlled so that they do not reduce water quality
• The precautionary approach to pollution should promote clean technologies and ban the discharge of synthetic substances until their long-term impacts are known.

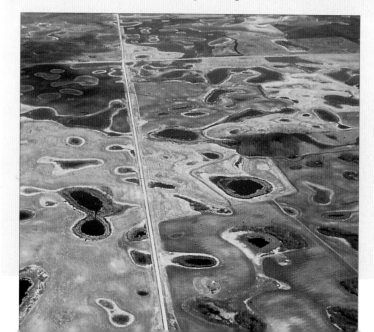

5

Integrate development of water resources with conservation of key ecosystems

Natural ecosystems are an integral part of the water cycle in each drainage basin. They both affect and are affected by the quality and quantity of water flow. Sustainability calls for:
• Good knowledge of how water and land use affect ecosystem functioning
• Preservation of watershed forests, lakeside and riverside vegetation and major wetlands of importance in regulating water movement and quality
• Full examination of the potential costs, benefits and environmental impact of all large water management projects, especially dams
• Restoration of critical forest and aquatic ecosystems that have been degraded or destroyed by human activity.

6

Prepare for major pollution accidents

Severe pollution incidents can result from floods, earthquakes and industrial accidents. The procedures for avoiding and responding to accidents include:
• Enforcement of strict safety regulations
• Provisions to protect water storage structures from contamination
• Establishment of comprehensive contingency plans
• Preparation of emergency clean-up and pollution containment services.

7

Promote community-level management of water resources

Government agencies should treat local communities as partners in water-resource management. They should foster both direct management by user groups and local associations, and greater participation in decisions on policies and programmes. Key areas for community action include:
• Local programmes to provide safe drinking water and to improve the provision of sanitation
• Management of, and priority access to, fisheries by artisanal fishing communities
• Local management of water harvesting and storage in drought-prone areas
• Operation of small irrigation systems by farmers' groups.

8

Strengthen international co-operation

Competing demands on water resources, transboundary pollution and the need to share information on water and aquatic ecosystems call for amicable co-operation between nations. There is scope for:
• More regional institutions set up to manage transboundary waters and resolve disputes
• The development of strategies and action plans to address priority problems such as severe pollution and falling ground water levels
• Increasing support for and strengthening of the Ramsar Convention, which covers wetlands of international importance, with assistance channelled to lower-income countries to help them conserve designated wetlands.

9

Protect rare or threatened aquatic species

Fresh waters support many plants, fish and invertebrates that are endemic to specific sites or river basins. To help protect aquatic life:
• Water pollution should be strictly controlled and kept to a minimum
• Fishing and harvesting of threatened species of animal or plant should be banned or strictly controlled
• All water engineering projects should be assessed for their potential impact on aquatic species, and measures taken to ensure they do not reduce the biodiversity of the areas they affect
• Introductions of exotic species should not take place without prior analyses of their likely impact on native species.

Left Part of the prairie potholes region – an area of more than four million small lakes, very important for wildlife – in Manitoba, Canada.

Above Community action builds a water cistern as part of Lake Nakuru Conservation and Development Project in Kenya.

Oceans and Coasts

The oceans are the dominant feature of our planet, covering the greater share of its surface, and playing a key role in the hydrological cycle, the chemistry of the atmosphere and the shaping of climate and weather. Long a source of food, a network of shipping lanes and a playground, the seas have more recently become suppliers of energy, minerals and medicines. These many contributions to the human economy are set to grow as technology advances and the resources of the land become more scarce.

The seas can seem to be strange and exotic. Many marine creatures are quite unlike those on land. The very unfamiliarity of names such as comb jelly, endoproct and kinorhynch testifies to the mystery of marine life. Most people are unaware of how they benefit from the oceans or of how oceans affect them. The science and management of the seas have become the job of a few specialists. But they must in future be the concern of us all. The vastness of the oceans suggests that people cannot harm them – the reality is rather different.

Above and above right Illuminated by the photographer's light, a coral shrimp is revealed in the strange and exotic world of the coral reef. Nusambier Island, Indonesia, is a patch of vivid green surrounded by coral and the seemingly endless blue of the sea.

Right middle Coral reefs form a vast variety of spaces and surfaces that other plants and animals can exploit as habitats. Powered by strong tropical sunlight, coral reef ecosystems are the richest in numbers of species and the most productive of all the marine ecosystems.

Bottom right A fisherman carries home his catch along a beach in Madagascar. Small-scale fishing in coastal shallows accounts for about 20 per cent of seafood production, but subsistence fishing is threatened by increases in human population along coasts.

The ocean world

The overwhelming importance of the oceans to the biosphere arises from several factors. The first is their tremendous size – oceans occupy 70 per cent of the Earth's surface. Second, being below the land, they serve as the sink for everything that is carried to them by water and air. Third, the contact between oceans and atmosphere provides a vast space from which water can evaporate and through which atmospheric oxygen and carbon dioxide are absorbed. Finally, the oceans are fluid and forever in motion.

The movement of the sea is one of its most important features. As well as the incessant action of the waves and the rhythmic ebbing and flowing of the tides, the whole water mass is in continual flow as part of the global system of oceanic circulation. Currents, like rivers in the sea, flow great distances and influence climates and both aquatic and terrestrial ecosystems. Where a warm and a cold current meet, as off the south and east coasts of Newfoundland, the waters tend to well up and mix, improving the circulation of nutrients and creating conditions in the top layer of the sea that are especially favourable for marine life.

The seas are inhabited by many different organisms. While the animals are often the most conspicuous of these, it is plants that comprise the bulk of living tissue. Phytoplankton – microscopic plants that float and drift in the surface layers of the water – are the basic producers in the ocean, as are the green plants on land. They are the foundation for marine life feeding the ocean ecosystem with the energy they absorb from sunlight. Zooplankton, tiny animals that drift with them, include representatives (as larvae or as adults) of many groups of animals. The larger and more familiar animals of the marine environment include crustaceans (such as shrimps, lobsters and crabs), molluscs (squid, octopus, clams, oysters and mussels), echinoderms (starfish and urchins), sharks, fishes of all kinds and cetaceans (whales and dolphins). Less exclusively tied to the sea, but nonetheless fully dependent on it, are sea turtles, seals and numerous species of seabird.

Crowded coasts

The seas provide diverse environments for marine life, with water depth, temperature, salinity and clarity setting varying conditions. The depth at which light is adequate to support photosynthesis, the basic energy-providing process of life, is variable, but is not usually more than 60 metres (200 feet). Most organisms are therefore restricted to the upper layers, but there are species adapted to living far below, relying on organic matter drifting down from the sunlit levels.

In large part, the biological wealth of the oceans is concentrated along a relatively narrow strip formed by the continental shelves, coastal margins and estuaries. Here are the major fishing grounds, yielding more than 80 per cent of the world's fishing catch. The shallows and edges of the seas are also the areas of greatest dynamism. The recurring tides, the pounding waves and the flows of tributary streams build up and break down deltas, cliffs and beaches. Coastal marshes buffer the land from the effects of the sea and serve as spawning and nursery grounds for many marine species. Mangroves, dense forests of specially adapted trees that thrive in warm, shallow tidal areas, serve similar functions. So do seagrass and seaweed beds. Along many tropical coasts, a short distance offshore and just beneath the low-tide line, coral reefs occur. Built by millions of tiny, soft-bodied polyps, coral reefs provide a rich habitat for myriad fish and crustaceans and also protect the shores from the full force of the sea.

Six out of ten people live within 60 kilometres of coastal waters

Altogether, the coastal zone, between the seaward margins of the continental shelves, to a depth of about 200 metres (660 feet), and the inland limits of the coastal plains, at 200 metres above sea level, has the highest biological productivity on Earth. It is also home to most of the world's population, who depend on its resources and largely determine its state of ecological health. Six out of ten people live within 60 kilometres (40 miles) of coastal waters, and two thirds of the world's cities with populations of 2.5 million or more are near tidal estuaries. Within the next 20-30 years, the population of the coastal zone is projected almost to double. These pressures, along with the impacts of expected climate change and sea level rise, will have major effects on the coastal zone. It may well be the main arena in which the efforts to create a sustainable society will take place.

The tide of deterioration

As a result of human activities, both inland and in the coastal zone itself, coastal and marine ecosystems and resources are rapidly deteriorating in many parts of the world. Urban, industrial, agricultural and tourist developments are often poorly planned and regulated. Engineering and development projects are modifying coastal ecosystems on a very large scale. The coastal zone is also affected by changes in salinity and sedimentation resulting from the damming of rivers and siltation due to changes in land use.

Marine pollution is steadily increasing. More than three quarters of it comes from land-based sources, by way of rivers, direct discharges and the atmosphere. The rest of the pollution comes from shipping, dumping and offshore mining and oil production. More than 90 per cent of all chemicals, refuse and other materials that enter coastal waters remain there in sediments, wetlands, fringing reefs and other coastal ecosystems.

Human inputs of nutrients into coastal waters already equal natural sources. Within 20–30 years they are projected to exceed the natural level by several times. The result will be a considerable extension of the kind of impact – the cycle of rapid algal growth, deoxygenation of water and ecosystem collapse – now found only in enclosed areas such as the Baltic Sea. Pathogens from sewage also pose health risks to bathers and to consumers of seafood. In many areas, stocks of shellfish have been declared unfit for human consumption.

Organochlorines, other synthetic organic chemicals and heavy metals are the most widespread and serious chemical pollutants. In addition, plastic and other debris such as pieces of nets, ropes, packaging materials, straps and rings entangle and kill marine mammals, turtles, fishes and birds, litter shallow waters and beaches, and are found even at abyssal depths.

Exploitation of resources

Despite these impacts, the world marine fish catch increased steadily during the 1980s, reaching 84 million ton(ne)s a year in 1988. However, it is not expected that, even in the long term, the total will rise above 100 million ton(ne)s. Most bottom-dwelling fish stocks are now fully fished, and much of the increase of the 1980s was from bigger catches of shoaling surface fish such as Peruvian anchovy, Japanese sardine and Antarctic krill, whose populations are highly variable. Indeed, overexploitation, facilitated by new technology, has led to the decline of many fisheries and greater instability in others. Competition is growing between small-scale, large-scale and sport fishing.

Many fisheries are also being put at risk by habitat degradation along coasts. Species that spend their young stages in brackish or fresh water are particularly vulnerable. There is competition between fishing and fish-farming. Badly sited aquaculture has severely damaged habitats – shrimp farming, for example, has devastated mangroves, which are themselves important nursery grounds for shrimps and various species of fish. A common problem with aquaculture is the spread of pests and diseases, which poses a serious risk to wild stocks.

Marine resources are usually treated as communal or state property. The ocean beyond 200 nautical miles (230 miles, 370 kilometres) from coasts still has no effective legal regime to regulate its use. Establishing Exclusive Economic Zones (EEZs) – out to 200 miles from shore – brought resources under the control of states. But even within their EEZs, most countries fail effectively to control access to and use of living resources. Many nations have ratified conventions on regional seas and fisheries, and other agreements on coastal and marine ecosystems, but most lack the programmes, institutions or resources to fulfil their obligations.

Right A pipe pours waste onto a beach, from where it will run into the ocean. It was once thought that the oceans were so massive that they could absorb and render harmless any pollution. This idea is now clearly false, with countless instances of damage to marine life.

Below Sockeye salmon jumping up falls in Katmai National Park, Alaska. Sockeye salmon live most of their adult lives in the ocean, but enter rivers and swim upstream to breed in freshwater. They are thus reliant on having both healthy rivers and seas.

Integrated management

The challenge for management is to use the resources and services that are provided by the oceans and seas to meet development objectives without degrading the the environment or exhausting stocks of living resources. At present, national policies for conservation and resource management tend to neglect the marine environment. Marine ecosystems and resources do not feature widely enough in planning programmes for economic development, pollution control, and establishment of protected areas and development control. All activities, regardless of how far inland, should consider the need to protect the oceans. The limiting of land clearance and of deforestation upstream, for example, can reduce problems caused by sedimentation around river mouths.

Above right A dead sperm whale on a beach in New York State, USA. The Whale's jaw is broken because it became entangled in a length of plastic rope. It is not only chemical pollution of the sea that causes damage to marine life. Discarded objects cause terrible injuries and death.

Right Windsurfers racing before a steady breeze. Protection of the marine environment is important to many people not only as an ecosystem and a resource, but also as a source of enjoyment and relaxation, and for its aesthetic value.

The United Nations Convention on the Law of the Sea

The United Nations Convention on the Law of the Sea (UNCLOS) would be the first comprehensive, enforceable international environmental law, covering all forms of marine pollution (land-based, atmospheric, ship-borne and that originating from activities on the sea bed). It takes an ecosystem approach to all uses of the oceans, offers an institutional framework for international, scientific and technological co-operation, and provides a binding system for the peaceful settlement of disputes.

Although some 45 nations are applying for the treaty, it is not yet in force, since this requires ratification or accession by 60 states. The combined efforts of international diplomacy, non-governmental organizations, citizens' groups and the UNCLOS Secretariat itself are needed to persuade nations that have not yet done so to commit themselves to the Convention.

Coastal management

Comprehensive coastal zone planning and management would benefit all seaboards, but priority could be given to areas with dense and increasing populations. Other priority areas would be where there are intense, conflicting pressures on coastal and marine resources, and seaboards where over-exploitation, pollution or habitat loss have had a major impact on resources.

Comprehensive planning can counter problems like shoreline instability and the settling of deltas during extraction of groundwater. In protecting shores that are vulnerable to sea level rise or storm surges, it is best to maintain habitats such as mangroves, mudflats and coral reefs, and processes such as sedimentation and marsh growth, that defend coasts. In some cases, modest engineering works may be justified to protect shores. In others, changes in land use may be required. Only where major population centres are threatened should substantial engineering works be considered.

The management of fisheries and other marine resources tends to be narrow in approach. Given the need to understand the natural fluctuations of fish stocks and their relationship with environmental factors, the focus of management should be shifted towards entire ecosystems. It should also give more weight to the interests of local communities with a tradition of resource management, and which directly suffer the problems of over-exploitation and ecosystem degradation. Small-scale, community-based fisheries account for almost half the world fish catch for human consumption, employ more than 95 per cent of the people in fisheries and use only 10 per cent of the

**All development
should consider the need
to protect the seas**

energy of large-scale corporate fisheries. However, governments often encourage large-scale and sport fisheries at the expense of small-scale fisheries.

When there is great pressure on coastal resources, particularly in densely populated areas, it is often necessary to reduce access to fisheries and develop other means of livelihood. Aquaculture is one option. It can be appropriate if a low-input system is used (small ponds, pens or tanks) so that it can be taken up by local communities, and if it does not harm the conservation of wild species.

Above Partially dried fish on a beach in the Banc d'Arguin National Park, Mauritania,. Since the emergence of humankind, people have reaped the bounty of the oceans, skimming the top of marine food chains. Salt water fish preserves well with the application of heat and strong ultraviolet light. For thousands of years, natural fermentation has been used to produce nutritious fish paste.

Ecosystem protection

Conservation of marine ecosystems requires a much more extensive network of protected areas – at present, marine reserves lag far behind their counterparts on land. Marine protected areas can serve as replenishment areas for fisheries and should be designed to maintain the maximum diversity of their ecosystems. Each protected area should have a management plan that integrates all uses of the waters, as pioneered by the Great Barrier Reef Marine Park Authority in Australia.

Strict protection of key threatened species, such as the great whales, monk seals, dolphins and sea

Conservation of marine ecosystems requires a much more extensive network of protected areas

turtles, remains a high priority. In many cases, this requires not just protection from hunting but protection of vital habitats, such as nesting beaches and breeding sites, from destruction or disturbance. The potential of aquariums to serve as ex situ gene banks, particularly of rare invertebrates, should be explored.

Tackling land-based pollution of seas and marine ecosystems requires rigorous control over the use of pollutants such as herbicides, pesticides, nitrate and phosphate fertilizers and synthetic organic chemicals. Special attention should be paid to improving sewage treatment in order to reduce the risks to public health from bathing in contaminated water and eating contaminated seafood. Much more work is needed in the development of water-quality criteria and effluent standards, particularly in tropical regions.

Pollution at sea has been addressed by current international agreements, especially the International Convention for the Prevention of Marine Pollution from Ships (MARPOL), which has reduced oil pollution and the dumping of toxic materials. However, much still needs to be done. Discharges of oil by tankers account for the largest source of oil pollution and could easily be prevented if MARPOL were properly enforced.

International obligations

The UNCLOS would oblige states to co-operate to conserve the living resources of the oceans. However, no existing international mechanism provides sufficient direct control of resource use on the high seas. Conflicts over unregulated driftnet fishing illustrate the need for an international management regime to ensure that uses of the open ocean are sustainable.

States should also adhere to regional conventions and consider new agreements. Regional plans are conspicuously absent for the Arctic Ocean, Black Sea, South Asian seas, North Pacific, Southwest Atlantic, South China Sea and the Sea of Japan. Regional fishery bodies could promote co-operation in research and development, including exchange of data on stocks, catches and landings, and organize the allocation of shared stocks. Since the declaration of EEZs, countries have been more protective of their data and have reduced the effectiveness of international organizations.

Better interdisciplinary research would further conservation by integrating the studies of specialists such as oceanographers, meteorologists, ecologists and social scientists. Development assistance agencies and research institutions in high-income countries should assist lower-income countries to strengthen their marine science capabilities.

Left Emptying the net of an ocean-going trawler before dropping it over the side to gather another load of fish. Overfishing by commercial fleets has in many cases led to drastic declines in fish stocks. Some countries, however, refuse to abide by quota systems that restrict catches.

Below Ropes and nets made from plastic mark this scene as modern, but otherwise the picture is almost timeless. Low-energy fishing has sustained human life for millennia, and with proper controls, protection and mangement can continue to do so indefinitely.

Priority Actions

2

Co-ordinate inshore management and land use in the coastal zone

Activities on land and sea bordering the coast have great influence on one another and on both land and sea ecosystems, and should be managed on an integrated basis. Coastal zone land-use and management plans should:
• Be organized according to the location of drainage basins and adjacent continental shelf ecosystems
• Include comprehensive planning of waste management to minimize harm to the environment and human health
• Regulate agriculture and other land uses to control erosion and siltation, and prevent chemical contamination
• Include components at both local and regional levels.

1

Raise the profile of coastal and marine issues

Governments, citizens' groups and the media can greatly increase awareness of the importance of the sea for all people and of the mounting threats to the coastal zone in particular. They should promote widespread understanding of:
• The contribution of the oceans to planetary life-support systems
• The vulnerability of coastal ecosystems to the impacts of actions inland
• The risks to public health from the contamination of coastal waters and seafood, often by sewage
• The nature of property rights in the coastal and inshore marine environment, and the need for limitations on fisheries, fish farming and other exploitation
• The need for legislation on the prevention of pollution, the sustainable management of resources and the protection of ecosystems.

3

Improve management of fisheries

Fishery policies need to increase support to community-based fisheries and to adopt an ecosystems approach to resource management. They should:
• Allocate user rights more equitably between small-scale and large-scale fishing fleets
• Improve the management of sports fisheries by ensuring catches are measured and regulated
• Explore the potential for local communities to manage coastal resources
• Provide community organizations with education and training in conservation
• Promote management of fishery resources based on estimates of their size and distribution, natural fluctuations in population size and interactions with other species
• Undertake continual studies to make such evaluations more accurate.

Above **Students studying mangroves in Bako National Park, Sarawak, Malaysia. Coastal wetlands are highly productive ecosystems that are easily exploited. While working to conserve as many areas as possible in their natural state, we must also accept that** others will inevitably be altered by use. By studying natural systems, we can learn to cause as little damage as possible. At present, too little is known about the workings of marine ecosystems, and the knowledge that we have gained is not widely enough shared.

4

Promote marine protected areas

The world-wide network of coastal and marine protected areas is underdeveloped. Governments should accelerate the establishment of protected areas and should in particular:
• Develop an overall national scheme to safeguard representative coastal and marine ecosystems, complemented by regional schemes
• Prepare management plans for individual protected areas, where possible integrating them into planning for coastal activities in general.

5
Conserve key and threatened marine species

Concerted action is needed in specific cases to conserve marine biodiversity and to save endangered species. Priorities include:
• Maintaining the present moratorium on commercial whaling to allow whale populations to recover fully
• Protecting major turtle nesting beaches from development and encouraging local communities to conserve turtles
• Controlling or banning fishing methods with a large effect on non-target species, notably dynamiting, the use of long drift nets and the use of non-degradable traps
• Preventing the accidental introduction of exotic species into new marine habitats (for example, by way of ships' ballast water) and ensuring no deliberate introduction takes place without prior analysis of the likely effects and without widespread approval.

6
Reduce marine pollution from land-based sources

Control of land-based pollution requires major changes in agricultural and industrial practices, as well as the development of better waste treatment technology and facilities. The main changes needed are:
• Comprehensive control of sewage
• Reduction in the run-off of fertilizers and livestock wastes through high standards of land husbandry
• Limitation of industrial effluents through more efficient use of resources and cleaner production technology
• Bans on disposal of all kinds of plastic.

7
Reduce pollution from ships and offshore installations

Current international agreements need stricter enforcement, along with provision of new guidelines. In particular:
• Operational discharges of oil by tankers should be stopped
• Educational campaigns should be mounted to encourage the owners and crews of ships to dispose of plastics and other synthetic materials safely – all ports should establish facilities for the reception of ships' wastes
• Plastic packing materials should have degradable sections to reduce the risk of trapping sea animals
• Contingency plans and procedures should be laid down to enable rapid response to emergencies such as oil spills.

8
Expand international co-operation

International co-operation on marine matters needs to be expanded and strengthened, both regionally and on a global scale. Nations should:
• Form appropriate regional bodies to manage shared ocean resources and problems, with adequate funds for regional seas programmes
• Enhance scientific co-operation and interdisciplinary research focused on an ecosystems approach
• Ratify or accede to the UNCLOS convention and other international legal instruments for protection of the oceans
• Promote the development of an effective regime for sustainable use of open-ocean and deep sea-bed resources
• Press for a moratorium on exploitation of newly discovered marine resources until adequate provision can be made for their conservation.

Above left Slowly a leatherback turtle walks back to the sea having laid eggs on a beach in French Guiana. After they hatch, the young turtles will also take to the sea, voyaging for thousands of kilometres across the oceans. Years later, those females that survive will return to this same beach and lay their eggs. This will continue so long as the turtles are left in peace. All species of marine turtle are endangered by a combination of natural predation, illegal hunting, the disruption of nesting beaches and increasing marine pollution.

Air and Atmosphere

The Earth's atmosphere is a blanket of gases 60 kilometres (40 miles) thick. It envelops the Earth and makes it fit for life. Millions of years of natural modification by volcanic outpourings and the physiological processes of living organisms have created the mixture of gases present today: the mixture we call air. Almost four fifths of the mixture is nitrogen. Oxygen makes up little more than one fifth, while the concentration of a dozen or so other gases, including water vapour and carbon dioxide, is only about 1 per cent.

The physical and chemical properties of the atmosphere protect and sustain the biosphere. The atmosphere traps some of the radiant heat of the Sun, maintaining a range of temperatures on Earth within which life can survive. This natural heat-trapping process is often termed the "greenhouse effect". A thin layer of ozone high in the stratosphere protects life further by screening out the dangerous ultra-violet radiation of the Sun. The air is the main source of oxygen, a requirement of almost all animal life. It is the reservoir from which plants take carbon dioxide for photosynthesis and from which bacteria fix nitrogen (essential for building proteins) in the soil.

Weather and climate

The atmosphere is a fluid, dynamic medium, which varies in temperature, density and humidity. Because the atmosphere is fluid, changes occurring at one point may spread over great distances. Variations in the condition of the atmosphere within a few days or weeks determine weather: the pattern and speed of winds, temperature, the build-up of moisture in clouds and its release as rain, fog, hail or snow. The pattern of variations over longer periods is described as climate.

Weather can be very changeable, and occasional events, such as wind and rain storms that exceed average severity, can cause floods, destroy buildings and result in the loss of human life. Extremes of high or low temperature can also cause death and destroy crops.

Climatic regimes, by contrast, are relatively stable and many human activities, such as growing crops or building houses, are geared to take full advantage of, or to secure protection from, prevailing climate. Nevertheless, changes in climate have taken place in the past over long periods of time. Global temperature changes of one to two degrees have generally occurred over periods of 1,000 to 10,000 years. Evidence from deep sea sediment cores and other sources indicate that during the last million years great ice ages followed by warming periods have recurred in cycles of about 100,000 years. Within those major cycles there were lesser ones; the most recent significant ice age ended about 10,000 years ago.

The atmosphere may seem vast, but it is not immune from disturbance. As human numbers and activity have grown, the composition and so the processes of the atmosphere are showing greater signs of modification. The most obvious changes are local and at a low altitude – the problems created by air pollution. But recently changes have been observed on a much wider stage.

Temperatures and ozone

Since the late nineteenth century, the world's average temperature has increased by about half a degree. Five of the warmest years on record were in the 1980s. Most atmospheric scientists believe that we are experiencing an unusually rapid warming of the global climate and that this is a result of human activities, although there is uncertainty about the rate and degree of warming.

This change is attributed to increased concentrations in the atmosphere of what are known as "greenhouse gases" – among which are carbon dioxide, water vapour, methane, chlorofluorocarbons (CFCs) and nitrous oxides.

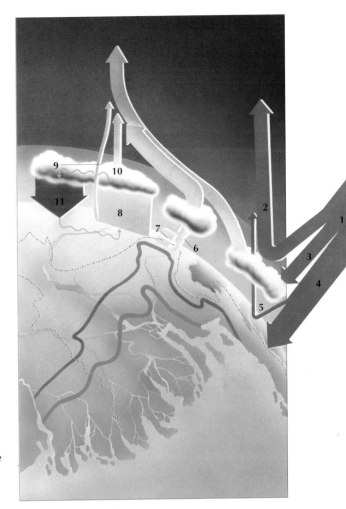

Right Greenhouse gases are fairly transparent to short-wavelength infra-red (heat) radiation, but tend to absorb longer wavelengths of infra-red. Heat from the Sun (1) has a short wavelength; some is reflected by the atmosphere (2), some absorbed (3), and some reaches Earth's surface (4). A small amount is reflected by the Earth (5), but most is absorbed. Some absorbed heat rises with heated air (6) or evaporated water (7). The rest is re-radiated from the Earth (8), but now as long-wavelength infra-red. A small amount escapes to space (9), but most is absorbed by greenhouse gases. Some of the heat in the atmosphere is radiated to space (10), but much is re-radiated downwards (11) to fuel global warming.

The green lines show what the effect of sea level rises would be in the low-lying areas around the Bay of Bengal. A 2 metre (6 foot) rise would reach the lighter line and a 5 metre (16 foot) rise would reach the darker line.

Above Tropical rainforest burning in Madagascar. Modifying the landscape in this way affects the air mass above. As well as releasing heat, carbon dioxide and other combustion products, the vegetation loss decreases the biosphere's ability to recycle water and carbon and generate oxygen.

Left A rice plantation at Cibodas, Indonesia. Tropical wet rice farming is one of the most highly productive methods of agriculture. There is, however, an invisible danger. Rice paddies are a considerable source of atmospheric methane, one of the "greenhouse gases" that increase global warming.

Although the concentrations of these gases in the atmosphere are tiny, even small increases reduce the passage of heat from the Earth through the atmosphere to space. Thus they cause the atmosphere and the Earth's surface to become warmer.

Complex, imperfectly understood interactions between atmospheric temperatures, concentrations of water vapour and the reflective effects of clouds make it difficult to predict the extent and timing of global warming with certainty. There is, however, no doubt that growth in human numbers and activities is causing steady increases in the emissions of all the greenhouse gases.

Concentrations of carbon dioxide in the atmosphere, as measured in air bubbles trapped at different levels in the polar ice caps, show an increase since the beginning of the nineteenth century, and most pronouncedly since the middle of the twentieth century. These changes coincide with increases in human numbers and use of carbon-based fossil fuels. Carbon dioxide is also released to the atmosphere by the destruction of trees and other plants, which are, in effect, temporary stores of carbon. Altogether, human activities are thought to have raised the concentration of carbon dioxide by 27 per cent since the mid-eighteenth century. Over the

Human activities are thought to have raised the concentration of carbon dioxide by 27 per cent since 1850

same period, the concentration of methane has doubled, its rise largely due to increases in the area devoted to rice and in the numbers of livestock – both rice paddies and the guts of herbivores are home to bacteria that generate methane.

Although the likely degree of global warming cannot be predicted accurately, there can be no doubt that even very small changes in average global temperatures would have pronounced effects. Assuming, as seems possible, warming by an additional one degree during the next 40 years, we can expect a rise in sea levels of 17–26 centimetres (7–10 inches), which would significantly increase the vulnerability of low-lying coastal areas to flooding from storm surges. Storm surges themselves are also expected to be more frequent as a result of global warming, adding to the risks for areas with large populations and inadequate sea defences, such as the shores of the Bay of Bengal.

Below Burning tyres in a Polish field. Vehicle tyres are just one of many products that consume large amounts of energy and can generate considerable air pollution during their manufacture.

During their disposal, such products often release into the atmosphere additional quantities of dangerous pollutants when the various substances from which they are made break down.

As sea level rises, salt water will also intrude into coastal ground water systems, damaging agriculture and domestic water supplies. The rise in temperature is likely to influence global precipitation patterns – some areas adequately watered at present may experience chronic water shortage. This will change the limits and extent of natural ecosystems and require the choice of different crops.

In recent years, significant changes have also been recorded in the stratospheric ozone layer. Increased penetration of ultra-violet rays because of thinning of the ozone layer would adversely affect marine plankton and juvenile fish and the yields of sensitive crops such as tomato, soybean and cotton. Ultra-violet rays can also cause eye damage, sunburn and skin cancer in light skinned people, and can suppress the human immune system. During the 1980s there was a 5 per cent decline in the average ozone concentration over Antarctica, and a 4 per cent reduction world wide. The main culprits seem to have been CFCs, which are used in a variety of ways, including spray cans, refrigerators and transformers. They break down in the stratosphere and release chlorine atoms, each of which can destroy as many as 100,000 molecules of ozone. The reactions are slow and will not stop until the CFCs in the stratosphere are used up. However, with international agreement to eliminate emissions in the near future there is hope that the situation will not become intolerable.

Acid attack

Climate change and ozone depletion reflect the dispersal of pollutants throughout the atmosphere. Before they have a chance to be dispersed, high concentrations of gases can create localized, but more immediate, dangers. Those that cause the worst damage and loss of life are compounds of sulphur and nitrogen, often associated with hydrocarbons. Today, the combustion of fossil fuels for transportation, heating, power generation and industrial purposes is their principal source.

One of the most damaging types of pollution is acid rain, more accurately called acid deposition because it may also take place by way of fog and snow. Acid deposition arises mainly from the atmospheric mixing of sulphur oxides and water vapour. Deposited on the ground, the resulting acids pollute water and contaminate vulnerable soils, killing trees and aquatic life.

One of the most damaging types of pollution is acid rain

Left Skeletons of trees that have been killed by "acid rain" in the Appalachian Mountains, USA. Apart from disrupting ecosystems, acid rain also causes immense economic damage by destroying stocks of trees and freshwater fish, among other things.

Above A motorcyclist on a rural road in central Java masking his face against air pollution. Widespread use of the internal combustion engine in vehicles and agricultural machinery has produced dangerously high levels of air contamination in many parts of the world.

Damage to European forests by air pollution in recent decades has been estimated to cost about $30 billion per year. In 1989, half the trees in German forests suffered some defoliation; in Poland, 75 per cent showed some damage. Harm to fisheries in 2,500 Swedish lakes has been attributed to acidification. In the north-eastern United States, a survey of 219 lakes in the Adirondacks revealed acid damage present in about 50 per cent of them. Increased rates of leaching of metals, including such toxic substances as lead and mercury, also result from the acidification of lakes and rivers. Meanwhile, acid deposition speeds up the corrosion of materials used in buildings and other constructions. Extensive damage has already been done to many of the world's greatest cultural treasures including the Parthenon in Athens.

The problem of acid deposition is not confined to high-income countries. China is already the third largest emitter of sulphur dioxide in the world, and other east Asian countries are in the path of prevailing winds that carry pollutants from its major sources. As industrial development in lower-income countries proceeds, the problems are only likely to get worse.

Smog alert

Photochemical smog is another severe form of air pollution. The major component of photochemical smog is low-altitude ozone, which mixes with more than 100 other substances in the air to form a gaseous mixture that is toxic to most living organisms. Photochemical smog develops when nitrogen oxides, which are produced during the combustion of fuels (such as those used in automobiles), react in the presence of sunlight with volatile hydrocarbons that are released by the evaporation of solvents, fuels, cleaners and paints. Exhaust fumes from motor vehicles are particularly harmful because they usually contain at least a small quantity of evaporated unburnt fuel. Photochemical smog, like the pollutants that are dominated by sulphur compounds, irritates and may severely damage forests, crops and the respiratory organs of animals. Each exposure to such smog may not be lethal in itself, but a number of exposures over a period of time may have significant and severe cumulative effects.

Photochemical smog is mostly a problem in cities, particularly those located where the land formations and local weather conditions combine to trap gases over the urban area. The smog that regularly formed over Los Angeles was the first to achieve notoriety (in the early 1940s), but as the number of cars, trucks and buses has soared, the problem has become world wide.

In cities like Mexico City and Santiago de Chile, the levels of smog pollution have forced drastic adaptations to be made – limits on the number of motor vehicles that can be operated at any one time, and closure of schools during periods with high risks of severe levels of smog.

Lead is emitted to the air from a variety of sources, including vehicles and factories. Lead disrupts the functioning of red blood cells, the liver and kidneys and may damage the nervous system.

Particulate matter – that is, particles of dust, soot and ash – may be an important pollutant, not only because it may cause physical irritation, but also because it provides sites for chemical reactions between other pollutants.

Cleaner methods

Strategies for controlling pollution to maintain acceptable atmospheric conditions and air quality involve eliminating emissions of polluting substances, or reducing them to levels that are at least less hazardous. The most satisfactory way of doing so is to develop substitute processes or practices.

Much success has already been achieved by changes in industrial processes and technology. With decreases in the use of coal and the installation of greater numbers of dust removal facilities, particulate matter emissions have tended to decrease in recent years, particularly in upper-income countries. Some decades ago, concentrated, low-altitude pollution by sulphur oxides was a major contributor to respiratory disease in cities in north-west Europe and the industrial regions of north-eastern United States. For a number of reasons – the use of cleaner coal, the substitution of oil and natural gas for coal, and the advent of mechanisms for cleaning flue gases – this type of pollution is now less severe.

Above A solar energy collector at Auroville in southern India. The Sun's rays are gathered by a curved mosaic of mirrors, and reflected onto a collection device suspended at the point of focus. Within the collector, a volatile liquid is vaporised and circulated through a heat exchanger, where it is cooled and pumped back to the collector. The extracted heat (in the form of hot water) can be used for domestic or light industrial purposes.

Top right Wind turbines situated near Germany's North Sea coast generate subtantial quantities of electricity. Rising fuel costs and fears about pollution have led to greater interest in wind power. Although wind turbines are highly visible, they are clean and relatively cheap to install.

Right A coke works in northern England. The air pollution from the works affects not only local people – a few of whom are seen here trying to catch fish in a nearby pond. Some pollution may drift for hundreds of miles before falling to the ground as acid rain.

Making it happen

Whatever the technical means for reducing air pollution, there are three basic ways to encourage their adoption. The first is to make sure that the costs and risks of pollution are clearly understood. The more people recognize the costs and the need to reduce them, the more this conviction will become part of the political agenda. The second is to apply economic incentives that will make it additionally attractive for polluters to change their practices to those that are more broadly acceptable. The third is prohibition; society may decide that certain polluting practices are completely unacceptable and prohibit them by law.

Control of air pollution is not, of course, simply a matter of local concern, although the effects are often felt most strongly close to the point where pollution originates. We are now aware that air pollutants can be carried and cause damage over great distances, across Europe for example. Through the Economic Commission for Europe, a Convention on Long-Range Transboundary Air Pollution was negotiated, initially to relieve the problem of acid deposition in Scandinavia resulting from pollution originating in the United Kingdom and the Ruhr region of Germany.

The Vienna Convention for the Protection of the Ozone Layer marked a first step in the international control of air pollution in 1985. Its Montreal Protocol in 1987 and the London revisions of 1990 are aimed primarily at preventing the further deterioration of stratospheric ozone by CFCs, but will at the same time help limit the total build-up of greenhouse gases. Manufacturers in the high-income countries (the major producers) will be obliged to stop producing CFCs by the year 2000. The signatory countries also agreed to assist lower-income countries in producing substitutes.

At the Earth Summit in Rio in 1992, a Convention on Climate Change was signed by the representatives of 154 countries. The Convention established the principles that should guide efforts to reduce emissions of greenhouse gases. However, because of the significant economic implications of controlling the use of fossil fuels, agreement on the targets and schedules for reduction could not be reached. Negotiations on this matter will have to continue. Responsibility for reducing greenhouse emissions falls heavily on the industrialized countries, because they are the source of some three quarters of total carbon dioxide emissions to date, and they also have the economic and technical resources for corrective action. All should commit themselves to reducing their carbon dioxide emissions by at least 20 per cent (from 1990 levels) by the year 2005, and by 70 per cent by 2030.

Control of air pollution is not simply a matter of local concern

There are many more examples of changes that are either being adopted now or are under study. Lead emissions are decreasing in countries where increasing numbers of motor vehicles are adapted to run on lead-free fuel. The introduction of catalytic converters helps to reduce nitrogen oxide emissions. Improved engine design can also reduce the release of dangerous substances.

More significant improvements in motor vehicles can be expected, but another important aim is to reduce the overall consumption of fuel. Vehicles that consume much less fuel have been designed, but should become widely used. Also required will be more efficient and attractive public transport and alteration of working practices to reduce travel between work and home. Many ways to reduce the combustion of fuels for heating buildings can be and are being found. These mainly involve insulation and other construction features, but centralized heat production and distribution to housing units can also contribute, as can the properly managed use of solid waste as fuel.

In other industrial fields, the greatest promise lies in finding economic uses for polluting materials that are currently considered as waste. Examples include the manufacture of bricks from fly ash and the recovery of methane gas from landfills and waste water treatment plants.

Priority Actions

1

Protect the stratospheric ozone layer

Phasing out the production and use of CFCs and other ozone-depleting chemicals will not only protect the ozone layer but also eliminate one of the most powerful and long-lived groups of greenhouse gases. To achieve this:
• All governments should implement the provisions of the Montreal Protocol as revised in London in 1990
• High-income countries should assist lower-income countries to introduce substitutes for ozone-depleting chemicals.

2

Control pollution by sulphur oxides, nitrogen oxides, carbon monoxide and hydrocarbons

Europe and North America account for 80 per cent of the world's emissions of the pollutants that cause acid rain and photochemical smog. Some lower-income countries are also at risk. Action is necessary in the following areas:
• Governments should try to achieve international emissions targets for a 90 per cent reduction of sulphur dioxide (based on 1980 levels) and a 75 per cent reduction of nitrogen oxides (based on 1985 levels) by the year 2000. Eastern European countries will need special help to meet these targets
• Further reduction targets should be set for these and other effluents, and governments should report annually on national action to reduce emissions
• Work should continue on defining the tolerance of ecosystems to acid deposition and developing new controls to ensure these "critical loads" are not exceeded
• Governments in regions that lack agreements should consider adopting regional conventions on the prevention of transboundary air pollution
• Higher-income countries should increase their efforts in the development of cleaner technologies, and help with the transfer of such technology to lower-income countries
• All countries should impose the highest standards practicable to curb vehicle pollution. Catalytic converters are the best technology currently available, but industry should intensify efforts to produce less polluting engines and improve fuel efficiency.

Above Monitoring air pollution in central London, England. Reduction of harmful emmissions from vehicles is an urgent priority. As well as causing low air quality at ground level, vehicle emissions contribute significantly to global air pollution.

Right A cloud of photochemical smog hangs over Mexico City the world's largest centre of population and, in terms of air quality, one of the most unhealthy. With rapid increase in population, the city has been unable to curb the consequent rise in pollution.

4
Prepare for climate change

There is a broad scientific consensus that, even if action is taken at once to curb greenhouse gases, some warming of the Earth's climate is inevitable. To prepare for the changes, governments should:

• Review development and conservation plans to allow for changes in climate and sea level, for example, limiting development in low-lying coastal areas

• Prepare for likely changes in agriculture by assembling stocks of plants likely to be more suited to future conditions, reviewing irrigation schemes and guiding farming communities whose practices may have to change

• Adopt measures to protect low-lying coastal areas, especially by prohibiting the destruction of coral reefs, mangroves, dunes and other natural defences

• Review plans for dealing with emergencies and disasters.

3
Reduce greenhouse gas emissions

Climate change, induced by the addition of greenhouse gases to the atmosphere, is one of the greatest threats to sustainability. Action to limit it must focus on curbing emissions of carbon dioxide, methane, CFCs and nitrogen oxides. Technically feasible and cost-effective ways of reducing emissions of these gases include:

• Using publicity campaigns, regulations and economic incentives to promote more efficient energy use in homes, offices, industry and transport

• Developing and adopting solar and other renewable energy sources that have low environmental impact

• Reducing carbon dioxide emissions further by, for example, substituting natural gas for coal, eliminating the wasteful burning ("flaring") of gas during oil extraction, closing older and more polluting factories

• Maintaining forests and establishing plantations, because trees are major absorbers of atmospheric carbon dioxide

• Reducing methane emissions by, for example, recycling and incinerating refuse, and recovering methane from fossil fuel extraction and storage, landfills and waste water treatment.

Top Workers observe gas flares at an oil field. Burning off gas, (which is a valuable fuel) that has been extracted together with oil is not only highly wasteful, but produces atmospheric pollution that could be avoided.

Above A coral reef at Pingalap Island in Micronesia, Pacific Ocean. Coral reefs form important barriers that protect many low-lying coastal regions and islands from the oceans. Coral reefs are being increasingly degraded and destroyed by various factors such as pollution. With the increasing threat to low-lying regions from the sea-level rises that would accompany increasing global warming, protection of coral reefs is essential.

Expanding on the themes introduced earlier, this section looks at the directions that must be taken at the individual, local, national and international levels in working towards a sustainable society. The actions proposed should help to change attitudes and practices in people's daily lives, empower communities to care more for their environments, make governments more effective in integrating conservation and development, and forge a global alliance that is committed to achieving a sustainable future.

Left Children with saplings from a nursery in the Udzangwa Mountains, Tanzania.

Changing Attitudes and Practices

Left The Botanical Gardens, Harare, Zimbabwe. Such gardens have traditionally had a two-fold function, serving as centres for academic activity and as places for recreation. By combining these functions, and adopting a more active approach to visitors, such traditional collections can play an important role, providing information and helping to shape popular attitudes and awareness.

Sustainable living can be achieved. But if it is to become the norm rather than the exception, many people in all parts of the world must change their attitudes and practices, towards one another and towards nature. Bringing about such fundamental changes is the most important challenge of our time, and will not be something that can be implemented either easily or instantly.

People will give their ethical and practical support for sustainable living once they are persuaded that it is right and necessary to do so, once they have sufficient incentives and once they gain the required knowledge and skills. These conditions apply to all people in all societies. For the poor, support will also depend on improvements in the quality of life: how successful society has been in releasing people from the constraints of poverty, and in fulfilling the most basic needs for housing, health and education.

At present, society fails to give most people the motivation, understanding and knowledge that they need. Indeed, in most of the upper-income countries, and increasingly in other countries with growing economies, the most powerful influences on popular attitudes – advertising and entertainment – promote overconsumption and waste. To counter them, concerted efforts to persuade and inform citizens through campaigns, education and training are central to any strategy for sustainability. Such efforts may come jointly or independently from governments, citizens' groups, educational institutions, the media and businesses.

Campaigns and informal education

Pressure groups, fund-raising bodies, and development and aid organizations have mounted many public campaigns that are aimed at increasing awareness of particular social or environmental problems. Environmental groups have successfully raised concern about issues such as deforestation, the loss of biological diversity (particularly the conservation of certain endangered species, such as the great whales, gorillas and African elephants), local pollution and inappropriate development projects. The World Wide Fund For Nature (WWF), Greenpeace, Friends of the Earth and many other organizations have been very successful in raising funds for conservation.

Above A sign at the boundary of the Banc d'Arguin National Park, Mauritania, proclaims in French and Arabic the intention to protect natural resources and ensure the future of the country's wildlife. A reserve's main function is to protect endangered habitats and species, but it can also serve to instill national awareness of ecological issues and attract foreign visitors.

The most powerful influences on popular attitudes promote over consumption and waste

Humanitarian groups have helped create concern in the more wealthy countries over poverty, famine and lack of development elsewhere in the world. Groups such as CARE, Oxfam and World Vision have raised millions of dollars annually. Originally the money was raised just for humanitarian relief, but more recently for activities – that are best described as aimed at human development – that attempt to find longer term solutions to the problems of human suffering.

Though individual campaigns are important in tackling specific urgent problems and in generating funds, environmental and humanitarian organizations could now join forces in a long-term programme to promote wider social change, based on acceptance of the ethics for sustainable living. The aim would be to communicate the importance of sustainability in general through all kinds of media. These efforts might be better characterized as forms of "informal education".

While formal education is centred in schools and colleges, informal education can take place anywhere and in many ways: from parents to children (and vice versa); from newspapers and magazines, television, radio, entertainment, advertisements; and from facilities such as museums, zoos and botanical gardens. Organizations concerned with promoting the change to sustainability need to use the full range of media. In areas where literacy is low, face-to-face and audio-visual means of communication may be important. In all cases, campaigns should encourage a two-way flow of information, enabling people to contribute as well as receive ideas and information.

To enhance the coverage of sustainability issues in newspapers, magazines and broadcasting, it is important to develop contacts with journalists and editors and to provide information they can readily use. In Pakistan, a Journalists' Resource Centre within IUCN's Country Office has been established as a specialist source of environmental information. Information summaries could also be targeted at other key communicators in society: teachers, labour unions, business groups, government officials and politicians.

More and more, informal and formal education are taking place together as environmental organizations collaborate with schools and education departments. In fact, the line between the two is unimportant except for administrative purposes. Significant contributions to both are being made by the Centre for Environment Education in Ahmedabad, India. The Centre has prepared a database of over 600 entries that teachers can use in preparing educational programmes. It has also produced *Joy of Learning*, a set of three handbooks of environmental education activities suitable for different age groups on which teachers can model class projects. The Canadian Wildlife Federation sponsors a nation-wide wildlife conservation art competition for school children in primary grades. This offers opportunities for learning and the chance to have achievements recognized.

Above A student field trip in Tanzania, East Africa, pauses to observe the behaviour of a herd of elephants. Such education not only increases knowledge, but also improves awareness of the value of the elephants as part of the natural environment and as an element of cultural heritage. This awareness can then be passed on by the students to other sections of the community. The passing of knowledge from people who have received education to others can be an important part of education campaigns.

Above Students on a Range Management Course, Mweka College, Tanzania, measure for themselves the amount of forage that is available at a particular location and season. In the future, as graduates, these students will put their education to practical use, working to achieve a balance between the demands of conservation, and the necessity of introducing sustainable methods of agriculture.

Formal education

The need for universal education has been stressed in earlier chapters. Formal education should not only be provided more widely but also changed in content. Children and adults need schooling in the knowledge and values that will allow them to live sustainably. This requires environmental education, linked to social education. The former helps people to understand the natural world, and to live in harmony with it. The latter imparts an understanding of human behaviour and an appreciation of cultural diversity. To date, this blend of environmental and social education has not been widely applied. It needs to be, at all levels.

Environmental education is still an evolving practice. Being dynamic, it is open to new information and concepts; it is also pragmatic and adaptable, focusing on the understanding and solution of real-life problems. Many jurisdictions now require their schools to offer environmental education but leave it up to individual communities to decide how they will handle the topic. One common practice is for students to undertake projects related to a course framework of natural science and social studies. Teachers can work together to incorporate environmental topics into their various courses in this way. In the longer term, environmental education could become a standard part of the training of teachers.

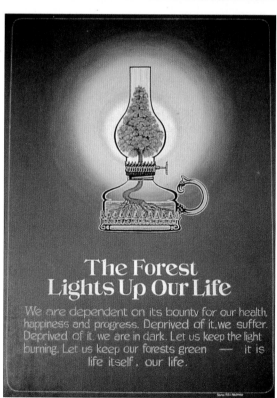

The Forest Lights Up Our Life

We are dependent on its bounty for our health, happiness and progress. Deprived of it, we suffer. Deprived of it, we are in dark. Let us keep the light burning. Let us keep our forests green — it is life itself, our life.

Examples of environmental education projects show how they can be both innovative and influential. Secondary school students in a Norwegian city brought about a noticeable change in buying behaviour when they analysed shoppers' preferences in detergents, and at the same time provided information on the environmental effects of phosphates. Students in four Italian schools undertook chemical, bacteriological and microplankton analyses of surface and ground waters in their local environment and submitted reports to the authorities and other concerned persons.

Persuading schools to take environmental education on board is not always easy, partly because it deals directly with values. Many school systems regard this as dangerous ground, and many teachers are not trained to teach values. The "whole school" approach, in which the school tries to behave consistently with what is taught, may also be dauntingly novel, but is important. Yet unless schools teach skills for sustainable living, conflicting values will continue to prevail. Development assistance agencies should give more support to environmental education. It is the key to sustainability. Where the significance of the environment is not understood, development will fail.

Where the significance of the environment is not understood, development will fail

Bottom left A wall poster at the Kerala Forestry Institute, southern India, uses an ancient metaphor to promote a positive attitude toward the environment. Without making any overt religious reference, the underlying message acknowledges and affirms a belief in the spiritual aspect of our living planet. Posters can be an effective element of informal education by spreading ideas to the widest possible audience.

Below With the guidance of a teacher, Madagascan children study educational material that has been produced and distributed by the World Wide Fund for Nature (WWF). International organizations have a major role to play in providing ecological information to schools and colleges. Many lower-income countries cannot afford to divert their scant educational resources into producing such material themselves.

Training programmes

In addition to general public education to create widespread acceptance of sustainable living, society also needs to provide specific training for workers in key environmental fields. More tertiary level courses and on-the-job training would help equip increasing numbers of specialists in areas such as ecology, resource management, environmental economics and environmental law. Many professions outside these fields also require a broader understanding than at present of how ecosystems and societies work, and of the principles of a sustainable society. Better support should be given to classes providing such training.

Training is vital not just for researchers, technicians and managers, but also for the direct users of resources. Farmers, fisherfolk, forest workers, artisans and other rural land and water users need the opportunity to learn how to use their resources sustainably and profitably. So do those of the urban poor who lack adequate utilities and must rely on their own efforts to manage resources as important as water supply.

Rural people would benefit from advice that combines information about sound methods of farming, soil and water conservation, sustainable production of fuelwood, timber and forage, sustainable management of wild resources and cottage industries. All would be helped by advice on development of income, self-help water supplies, sanitation, nutrition, family health, and cheap, environmentally sound technologies for housing, cooking, heating and other needs. Training can best come from well-trained extension workers – teachers and demonstrators working in the field – as well as from other extension services such as correspondence courses. It is most likely to be effective if delivered through a community-based organization. In many cases, advice will have to be closely integrated with efforts to extend credit and provide people with the land and materials that will enable them to change their practices. People will otherwise get frustrated by, and eventually ignore, ideas they cannot turn into action.

People could increasingly train each other, sharing all the knowledge that they already have. Communities across middle and low-income countries in particular need to exchange information on conservation and development projects, planning methods, training workshops, the distribution of training materials, local networks for sustainable development and effective communication. These exchanges could lead to the transfer of technologies for sustainable development directly between lower-income countries (so-called "south-south" as opposed to "north-south" transfers).

Priority Actions

1

Motivate, educate and equip people to live sustainably

Promoting sustainability means making full use of public campaigns and the educational system to explain why a sustainable society is essential and to provide all citizens with the values, knowledge, skills and incentives to help them achieve it and flourish in it. Such aims should be backed up by:

• A unified approach that covers informal education, formal education and training to ensure that they reinforce one another, for example, to avoid children being taught one thing in school only to be influenced to do quite the opposite by what they see and hear outside

• Use of the media as allies in promoting change, including the development of a corps of journalists and editors who are environmentally educated

• Systematic surveys designed to find out how well the principles of sustainability are understood, what people are willing to carry out (and pay for) and how satisfied they are with progress.

2

Campaign for a sustainable society

Transforming hard-set attitudes requires a concerted information campaign, encouraged by government and led by non-government organizations. The best methods will vary with cultural tradition, religion and stage of development, but the following guidelines are useful:

• Involve everyone; encourage new ideas

• Use all available media – print, radio, television, film, videotapes, posters, public meetings, theatre, street theatre, dance, song, traditional storytelling – according to audience

• Relate national and global issues to local situations, using familiar examples

• Get people to interact and discuss ideas for their local areas

• Make sure people have access to clear information on issues as well as advice and practical help on how to implement changes they devise for themselves

• Involve volunteers, especially children, in projects for their areas, such as restoring degraded land or planting trees

• Use information centres and exhibits, both within local communities close to home and in places people visit with the expectation of learning such as museums, zoos, botanic gardens and national parks.

Above Volunteer assistants and officials from the national conservation society record a discussion for local radio in Lusaka, Zambia. Later, the discussion will be broadcast as part of the radio service's

Chongolo Club of the Air, which provides a forum for discussion of environmental issues. The mass media provide the means to spread information to a wide audience, provoke discussion of issues and encourage co-operation.

Above right A poster produced by local forest-protection groups in Rio Branco, Brazil, a region on the front-line of the battle to preserve the Amazon rainforest. People opposing conservation is usually the result of ignorance.

4
Meet the training needs for a sustainable society

Governments, in partnership with the teaching profession, should determine the new combinations of professional and technical skills that a sustainable society will require:
• At the professional level, there will be great need for specialists in ecology, the various sectors of resource management, environmental economics and environmental law
• At the technical level, the main need is for more extension workers who are trained to understand ecological relationships and can help resource users to develop better practices through lessons, demonstrations and advice in the field. They should be able to give broad advice rather than focus on a single sector such as agriculture or fisheries
• Development assistance agencies should support action plans designed to meet those needs, and support efforts by grassroots groups to exchange personnel and information.

3
Make environmental education an integral part of formal education at all levels

Environmental and social education should be integral to primary and secondary schooling, and to many courses at higher levels. It is important that:
• Environmental themes are incorporated into all courses, although some specialist courses are needed, particularly at the tertiary level
• Environmental education is easily coupled with literacy programmes. By focusing on the daily lives of families and the resources on which they depend it can increase the immediate relevance and attractiveness of education, and so enhance enrolment. Formal education should not try to supplant, but work with, traditional educators
• Teaching in schools should include practical projects. Audits of the use of energy, paper and other resources in school can show ways of reducing consumption and costs without harming school activities. The lesson that sustainability pays will be taken home
• Teachers trained in the social sciences need to work closely with environmental educators, using their methods to build social awareness of the need for sustainability into their courses.

Above left A worker with the World Wide Fund for Nature (WWF) holds an impromptu meeting with Tuareg nomads near Aïr, Niger, to discuss the progress of a development project. Participation by those affected is a key element in sustainable development, as is passing on knowledge, whether through general environmental education or training for particular projects. Development workers can play a central role in these processes.

Above At Karnali in western Nepal, traditional tools and techniques are used to cut planks for local building purposes. This is timber use at a sustainable level, and can be supported through training.

Empowering Communities

Most of the creative and productive activities of individuals or groups take place in communities. Communities and citizens' groups provide the easiest means for people to take socially valuable action as well as to express their concerns. When they are properly empowered and informed, communities can contribute to decisions that affect them and play an indispensable part in creating a sustainable society.

The word "community" here means the people of a local administrative unit, such as an urban or rural municipality, of a cultural or ethnic group, or perhaps the people of a particular neighbourhood or valley. Some communities are much more distinctly defined than others and more cohesive. But even where the sense of community is not strong, co-operative action can still be highly effective.

The actions of communities are often readily channelled through the local governments that represent them. Local authorities usually have the responsibility for various aspects of environmental care, including land use planning, development control, water supply, treatment of waste water,

waste disposal, health care, public transport and education. But communal action through non-governmental bodies such as local citizens' groups and grassroots movements is equally important. Often these community groups can be more responsive to the changes needed to sustain productive local environments. They can work together with local authorities to enhance conservation action, pollution control, rehabilitation of degraded ecosystems and the improvement of urban environments. The sum of these and similar activities has been termed Primary Environmental Care.

Group action

Community groups concerned with environmental issues and sustainable development come together initially for a variety of reasons. Often they arise from efforts to prevent some change that will affect the community, such as a forest clearance or water development scheme that people regard as destruction of amenities and an untenable break with tradition or as a threat to their livelihoods. Having formed themselves for a defensive reason, they may later focus on more positive activities. Groups may also come together with more general aims of improving the environment and enhancing their opportunities for development.

Effective groups may act as a catalyst for the formation of others, and the number of such organizations in a country can grow rapidly. India's Chipko movement is one of the most famous community-based initiatives. It started in 1975 in a village in the foothills of the Himalayas when the women of the village ran ahead of loggers to hug the trees slated for felling. They succeeded in saving those trees, and today there are many Chipko groups actively engaged in reforestation, soil conservation and environmental education.

By 1988, Kenya was estimated to have 25,000 women's groups – an increase from only 4,000 in 1980. All are active in self-help activities, notably soil conservation and tree planting. Many started as savings clubs. One such, in the western village of Emulole, was started by women who wanted to save to send their children to school. The 48 participants work in teams on farms and put one third of their earnings into the group account. They use that capital to buy grain that they hold for sale when the price rises. Dividends are distributed to group members at the end of each year. The group has many ideas for additional activities, such as increasing the variety of crops grown and organizing training for young people, but they have many obstacles to overcome, not least the difficulty in securing enough money. At the same time they fear that if they seek external financial support, the price might be loss of control over the scheme.

Support for change

Because of a lack of money, a desire to maintain control or other reasons, governments at all levels sometimes fail to respond to community groups. However, the realization that actions at the grass roots can be broadly beneficial is bringing changes in the attitudes of governments. Official development assistance organizations and bodies such as Oxfam are also focusing more on communities.

Support for community-based action is critical. Communities need certain conditions if they are to care for their environments effectively. They need: secure access to land and resources, and an equitable share in managing them; education and training to build their knowledge, skills, self-confidence and self-reliance; rights to free speech, free assembly and full participation in decisions that will affect them (see box below); and adequate funds.

**Effective community groups
may act as a catalyst
for the formation of others**

Left A meeting of a Masai womens' co-operative, Kenya, where there are more than 25,000 womens' groups, all of them active participants in conservation programmes such as soil protection and tree planting. By encouraging such groups, governments can tap a powerful, effective and often under-utilized resource in the community.

Below A meeting attended by women of a village in Senegal. Discussion and decision-making at the community level are the primary ways in which individuals can express concern about issues that affect their lives. A united voice is also better able to express such concerns to local authorities.

Community participation

Facilitating community participation in government and other decisions helps to ensure that decisions are sound and that all parties will support them. Consultations should take place locally, involving the full range of community groups and organizations, as well as traditional leaders. Participants need adequate but readily intelligible information and enough time to be able to consider it, contribute to proposals themselves and respond to invitations to consult or ask questions. Care needs to be taken to ensure that consultations are in a culturally acceptable form. For example, indigenous people who have a tradition of decision making by means of communal discussion should not be expected to respond to a proposal by putting forward a written submission from one representative – if there are indigenous consultation mechanisms, they should be used. The timing of consultation is also of crucial importance. It should not take place so early that no useful information is available, nor so late that all people can do is react or object to detailed proposals already in the pipeline.

Land rights and participation

In many communities, people do not have sufficient land security. In such cases, government land-tenure reforms are essential. Hunters and nomadic herders need guaranteed access to hunting grounds and to grazing areas. Farmers, including shifting cultivators, require clear title to their land. In urban areas, the right to a house site is crucial. Land security gives people a stake in their own futures and so encourages sustainable actions.

Ensuring local participation in decision making means not just a token involvement, but accepting communities, who know their environment best and are directly affected by changes to it, as full consultative partners. In many cases, decisions could be devolved to them entirely, although safeguards are needed to ensure one community cannot eclipse the interests of others.

Participation also needs to be enhanced within communities. All members should play a role in decisions that affect their livelihoods, particularly in those decisions on the use and management of common resources. But some communities exclude women and ethnic or religious minorities from major decisions. In others, lack of cohesion and a sense of community means that a lengthy process of community-building may be necessary.

Fair returns

Local government and community organizations also need adequate funds and technical assistance for their sustainable development projects to begin. Central governments, official aid agencies or development organizations could provide financial help through credit and grants. Governments can also ensure that communities gain a fair return from managing resources sustainably or selling products produced sustainably. The government of Zimbabwe's Communal Areas Management Programme for Indigenous Resources (Campfire)

enables rural communities both to manage and benefit directly from the wildlife and any other resources in their regions.

Eventually, such projects are likely to become increasingly self-supporting. Sponsors – be they national governments, NGOs, academic institutions or the banking sector – should recognize that, like all paths to sustainability, community environmental action is based on changing attitudes and practices. It may not require a lot of money, but it will almost certainly need a lot of time. It can, however, yield highly rewarding results.

In Nepal, the Baudha-Bahunepati Family Welfare Project started in 1973 with the aims of lowering infant mortality, reducing population growth, raising agricultural productivity, conserving forests and providing community facilities such as drinking water and irrigation canals. It received support from several national and international NGOs, and now involves nearly 128,000 people. The project has been remarkable in mobilizing local people. The villagers bear much of the cost of public works by contributing their labour.

Above Tribal people in the Suleiman Mountains of Pakistan leading a way of life that has changed little for centuries. People in marginal lands long ago learned how to use their land sustainably. If they had not done so, the land would soon have ceased to support their ways of life.

Right Family group in Meka village, situated in the buffer zone around the Korup National Park, Cameroon. Buffer zones can protect traditional, sustainable ways of life as well as the reserves they surround, while at the same time allowing for well-managed development.

Indigenous communities

Left An encampment of the Dhangar people, nomadic shepherds in the Pune region of India. Laws in many parts of the world have tended to favour settled communities, and discriminate against nomads. It is essential that nomads are given sufficient land rights to continue their ways of life, especially in regions where the land will not support settled farming.

Some 200 million indigenous people (4 per cent of world population) live in environments ranging from polar ice and snow to tropical deserts and rain forests. They are distinct cultural communities with land and other rights based on historical use and occupancy. Their cultures, economies and identities are inextricably tied to their traditional lands and resources. Hunting, fishing, trapping, gathering, herding or cultivation continue to be carried out for subsistence – food and materials – as well as for income. They provide communities with a sense of continuity with the past and unity with the natural world, reinforcing ethics of sharing and of stewardship of the land.

It is often assumed that indigenous peoples have only two options for the future: to return to their ancient ways of life, or to become assimilated into the dominant society. They should, however, also have a third option: to modify their life styles, combining the old and the new in ways that maintain and enhance their identity while allowing their economy to evolve. Their chances of following such a path will be much improved if governments recognize aboriginal rights to use and manage land and resources, including the rights to harvest animals and plants on which they depend. People should participate in development decisions and have an equitable share of the proceeds.

Priority Actions

1

Provide communities with secure access to resources and an equitable share in managing them

Communities and individuals need long-term rights to the land and other resources necessary for their livelihood. Without them, people will not be motivated to use resources sustainably. The priorities for legislators and land management authorities are:

• Securing land rights for indigenous groups, farmers and urban dwellers
• Recognizing communal property rights and traditions of community resource management in legislation
• Intervening where necessary to ensure shared resources are managed co-operatively in the interests of all the community – and of other communities as in the case of migratory wildlife
• Supporting land rights by defining land holdings, legalizing tenure, improving the system of transfer and registration, and keeping records up to date.

2

Enhance participation in conservation and development

Local governments, community groups and other local interest groups should help to set the agenda for human development through strong participation. They should:

• Be full partners with central governments in making decisions on the policies, programmes and projects that will directly affect them and their local environments
• Where possible make the decisions themselves, without central government involvement, especially when dealing with projects that do not significantly affect the national interest
• Ensure that all sectors of the community have a chance to express and defend their interests
• Ensure that women can participate fully and contribute their expertise as environmental managers.

Above Pressed tight against an enclosing barbed wire fence, a squatter's house clings to a small patch of land in Esteli, Nicaragua. Such housing is often a consquence of failing to provide the land rights that are necessary for a settled existence.

Top right People collect water from a village well near Kumasi, Ghana. Facilities, such as safe supplies of water, can be created and effectively managed by community action. Access for all gives a common interest in ensuring success.

Right Oxleas Wood in the suburbs of London, England. The ancient woodland was defended fiercely by local groups when it was threatened by a road-building proposal. The combined voice of the community gave the protestors a national hearing.

4

Develop more effective local governments

Local governments are key units for environmental care. They are the tiers of government that are best able to understand the day-to-day needs of their citizens, that represent local people most directly, and with which citizens have most and more direct contact. They should be able to:

• Enforce land-use planning and pollution prevention laws, in accordance first of all with national standards, but with more stringent standards where local needs and interests so demand

• Ensure safe and efficient water supplies, sewage treatment and waste disposal for the areas they represent

• Regulate transport and local industry, again in accordance with national standards or higher

• Invest in and promote all aspects of environmental improvement.

3

Care for the local environment in every community

All communities should take action to care for their environment. They should be encouraged by governments (central and local) to debate their environmental priorities, and to develop local strategies for sustainability (for example, through workshops which could involve invited experts). In upper-income countries the aim should be to:

• Reduce resource consumption, waste and harmful impacts on the environment

• Restore local habitat and species diversity by e.g. cleaning up degraded urban and rural environments and creating local nature areas.

In lower-income countries:

• The focus should be on communal projects in agro-forestry, soil and water conservation, restoration of degraded land, low-cost water and sanitation provision, housing and infrastructure in villages and neighbourhoods

• Environmental action programmes should be combined with business development and help for people, particularly women, to obtain adequate education, training, primary health care and family planning.

5

Provide financial and technical support

Governments and development assistance agencies should support and enhance community environmental actions, with help in funding, expertise and technology. Support can also come from universities, banks, religious groups, environment and development NGOs, and national and international institutions. Governments can help with financing in many ways by:

• Guaranteeing low interest loans

• Matching funds raised by the community with grants coming from central coffers

• Developing tax concessions and subsidies that encourage people to make environmental improvements

• Ensuring communities earn a fair return for products derived from sustainably managed resources.

Providing a National Framework

Governments must lead the way to a great many of the changes that are advocated in this book. They have a pivotal role to play, because they have the power both to undertake large-scale projects directly and by various means to shape the conditions that either encourage or hinder the positive actions of citizens.

The way in which governments operate has a crucial influence on their ability to implement change. To achieve sustainability, societies need a national framework for the integrating development and conservation. There must be effective public institutions, comprehensive environmental laws and consistent social and economic policies, all backed up by a sound information base.

Integrated decision making

If sustainability is to become an overall aim of government, it must have an influence across the breadth of policy. The environment, after all, is the fundamental resource on which societies are built. It affects all sectors of activity, and any action that alters the environment is likely to have wide repercussions. At present, policy making tends to be fragmented, reflecting the division of government into isolated departments with limited mandates. Institutions set up to run environmental protection, for example, often have only weak links with resource management agencies (such as those managing fisheries), and their policies are seldom co-ordinated with the economic decisions that largely shape the environment. Such fragmentation hampers co-ordination of policies and increases the difficulty of resolving inter-departmental conflicts.

> **The environment is the fundamental resource on which human societies are built**

Much greater integration of policy and policy making is required. Inter-departmental units to examine the implications for sustainability of all policy and investment proposals would be highly effective. Such institutions should be closely associated with the central elements of government, such as those responsible for finances. An additional fundamental change at the operational level would be to make government agencies cross-sectoral. Each institution, for example, should combine responsibility for natural resource use, human development and resource conservation.

Through a cross-sectoral approach, governments will be best able to develop long-term strategies for sustainability. General strategies can then be translated into specific objectives through regional and local land-use plans. An integrated approach will also foster a government's ability to assess development programmes and projects for their likely environmental impacts, and it will also help to strengthen regulations designed to reduce hazards such as industrial pollution.

The legal framework

Law, in its broadest sense, is an essential tool for achieving sustainability. It sets standards of social behaviour and gives a measure of permanence to policies. The law can also require changes that vested or short-term interests would otherwise resist. Environmental law, based on a good scientific understanding and a clear analysis of social goals, can set out rules for human conduct that would, if followed, help communities live within the capacity of the Earth.

At the most fundamental level, a commitment to sustainability should be written into each nation's constitution or some other authoritative definition of a nation's means of government and policy. This basic commitment could then be put into effect by developing a comprehensive system of environmental legislation.

As a minimum, laws should be passed to cover land-use planning, pollution, energy use, resource use, waste and the conservation of species and ecosystems. Many of the laws should set minimum standards with which manufacturing industries, farming, fisheries and other activities have to comply, and should be based on what would be achievable using the best available technology.

It may be useful to phase in new standards that exceed the present capacity of industry, so that companies have a chance to develop the necessary technology before tighter legislation comes into force. Some laws will be concerned with licensing, auditing and monitoring, others with economic incentives. Penalties for contravening the laws must be stiff enough to ensure the laws are obeyed. The enforcement machinery must also provide for rehabilitation, or compensation for, damaged private or public property.

Local authority legislation also has an important role to play, since some areas may be more in need of environmental protection than others. While national standards should, whenever possible, be set and adhered to (and should reflect internationally agreed rules), states should accept that stricter measures may be needed at the local level.

Valuing the environment

Economics and law must work together. The law sets the rules and standards for upholding human rights, protecting the disadvantaged and the interests of future generations, and conserving the vitality of nature. The market ensures that society works within those rules as efficiently as possible. To do so, societies, and governments in particular, must ensure they assign realistic values to life-support services and natural resources – what we might term "environmental assets".

**We must assign realistic
values to life-support services
and natural resources**

Left Autumn colours in the Aletsch Reserve, Switzerland. The decision to create reserves often must be made at the national level, and needs suitable and sufficiently strong legislation to ensure that plans are effective. The creation of reserves usually involves various government departments and so is aided by a cross-sectoral approach.

Above A pollution control officer working for the National Rivers Authority of the United Kingdom measures water quality. The authority was set up by government to monitor and enforce water quality standards established by law. Such government institutions can be an essential part of successful environmental management.

At present, neither market, planned nor mixed economies take account of the full value of life-support systems and resources, or of the true costs borne by society if they are impaired or reduced, now or in the future. The general tendency has been to undervalue environmental assets or ignore them, undermining the case for their conservation.

If a natural wetland, for example, is assigned no economic value, then its conversion to arable land cannot be seen to have an economic cost. By the same token, society does not conventionally assign a value to such things as the shade of a tree on a city street, to a clean river, to fresh air, to reliable rainfall, to the untapped genetic resources of biodiversity, or to the natural pollination of crops by insects, bats and birds. Fortunately, this is beginning to change as attempts are being made to devise more comprehensive methods of valuation, using such concepts as full social cost (see page 27). These considerations have important implications for how governments judge economic performance and set policy priorities (see box opposite).

Although valuing environmental assets is a difficult and evolving process, it has already stimulated a number of techniques for taking unconventional values into account when assessing whether development projects (private and public) should go ahead. One of the most promising of the project appraisal techniques is Environmental Impact Assessment (EIA). An EIA simply widens the approach to decision making from a narrow focus on short-term economic gain.

To carry out an EIA is to define and appraise all the expected impacts of a proposed project on the environment, including water levels and quality, air quality, vegetative cover, farm products, animal populations, fisheries and the movement patterns of animals. Used in its widest sense, it might better be called "development impact assessment", since it examines social and economic consequences as well, such as short- and long-term employment, relocation of people and impacts on health. EIAs can compare the results of projects with the benefits forgone if projects do not go ahead. They can also form the basis of environmental management plans to mitigate the problems caused by projects deemed to be worth while. One of the benefits of an EIA is that it brings together a wide range of considerations before investments are committed.

Different governments have differing requirements for project appraisal, although some international organizations such as the United Nations Environment Programme and the World Bank are now encouraging movement toward common approaches. Meanwhile, increasing use of EIA and other techniques has already prompted some changes in the private sector. Many businesses have adopted the policy of anticipating what governments may require. Some industrial groupings have adopted codes of conduct that call on members to undertake comprehensive policy, process and product appraisals. Because they force careful examination of options, businesses frequently find them cost-effective in terms of profitability.

Measures of economic performance

Left Hyde Park in central London is a green island in a densely inhabitied urban landscape. Although city parks may not commonly be thought of in the same light as a nature reserve, they are nonetheless important environmental assets and should be protected as such.

Below A ship drowned in sand, a haunting image from what was once part of the Aral Sea, Uzbekistan (in the former Soviet Union). The sea has lost about two thirds of its area as a result of grossly misconceived government-planned irrigation schemes.

It is gradually being realized that standard calculations of a country's economic performance, such as gross national product (GNP) and gross domestic product (GDP), are less than adequate measures of a country's well-being, even in purely financial terms. The problem is that in conventional calculations the depletion of natural assets – forests and fisheries are two good examples – is not reckoned as a loss, but the sale of the products derived from them is considered as income. The calculations also take no account of human-induced soil erosion, losses of soil fertility and pollution, though these are likely to raise costs of production or result in lower yields for a range of human activities. In fact, the services rendered in counteracting environmental damage are actually recorded as income, not as expenses. For example, expenditure in cleaning up an oil spill is considered to be a contribution to GNP, while the environmental costs of the oil spill are not even taken into the equation. In all these examples, only cash flow is taken into account, yet clearly this is an inaccurate reflection of the real impact of the activities on a nation's assets and welfare, and therefore its future. A country may be heading for bankruptcy – depleting its mineral reserves, destroying its forests, polluting its air and waters, and spending the proceeds on current consumption – and still believe its economy is performing well because the GNP figure looks so good. Several countries, including France and Norway, are now attempting to refine a process of accounting that includes these factors and incorporates them in their national accounts. A key problem is the difficulty of evaluating environmental assets so that their values can be converted into monetary terms to enable proper comparisons with values resulting from market transactions.

Using economic instruments

Economic policy, realigned to take account of the full value of environmental assets, can be effectively directed towards sustaining ecosystems and natural resources. Economic instruments are valuable tools, first, because they provide a powerful incentive in themselves and, second, because at the same time they leave individuals and industries the freedom of choice as to the precise means they adopt to achieve the desired ends.

Instruments such as taxes, charges, subsidies, tradeable permits and performance bonds can help to correct biases that are caused by the market's under pricing of environmental assets (see box on previous page). In effect, such instruments use market forces in a way such that both producers and consumers are moved towards environmental objectives and so sustainability.

Right An ecologist takes a sample of marsh water for analysis. A essential element in improving the scientific understanding of ecosystems is obtaining sufficient data. National monitoring schemes are the best way to ensure that data are gathered effectively, with sufficient coverage of the whole range of national ecosystems.

Policies for sustainability must rest on a sound knowledge base.

Economic instruments are progressive in that they stimulate the development of sustainable technology and practice. They promote efficiency, reduce the costs of enforcing regulations and generate revenue. Through them, governments can implement the Polluter Pays Principle (see page 56) and its variant, the User Pays Principle (see page 39), making, for example, a timber industry bear the costs of any contamination, soil loss, irregular water run-off and loss of biological diversity that it causes, as well as of direct timber loss. The higher prices passed on to consumers can in turn stimulate the conservation of resources and the avoidance of goods that involve pollution.

The knowledge base

Without sound scientific knowledge, and public and official understanding of its implications, policies for sustainability are unlikely to be as well formulated or as widely supported as they should be. First and foremost, the information that is needed to integrate development and conservation depends on vigorous, comprehensive research. Universities and other research institutions in many countries have suffered from diminishing government support recently, particularly in terms of funding, and this trend needs to be reversed. This is especially the case in the area of environmental sciences. International co-operation is important for building the research capacity of lower-income countries.

Governments should establish, and continually review and improve, national monitoring systems. Continuous long-term series of data are essential. They should cover key indicators of environmental health, such as the status of natural resources (for example, the numbers of threatened species, changes in forest estate, water and air quality), and human development, such as life expectancy, literacy, the usefulness of laws and environmental measures, and changes in public attitudes. A global monitoring network is also needed so that national data sets can contribute to a global overview. Collaborative satellite monitoring systems are important for keeping check on the state of major ecological formations like forests and deserts and on worldwide changes in land-use patterns.

Above Red leaves in Corbett National Park, India. National parks and reserves are not only essential as means of preserving species and ecosystems. They are also important for research. Without knowledge of the working of ecosystems in their natural state, it is difficult to make effective decisions for improving the condition of damaged areas.

Economic instruments

Below An enhanced satellite image of Rondonia, western Brazil. Satellite monitoring is an important element in keeping a check on the state of the world's forests. The image shows an area of rainforest of around 240 kilometres (150 miles) square. The blue rectangles in the centre are evidence of commercial logging. The blue grid-like pattern to the lower right has been created by slash-and-burn agriculture.

Governments can employ a number of economic policy instruments to promote conservation and sustainable development.

• Resource taxes. Government taxes are useful for limiting consumption of resources like fossil fuels, to reduce both depletion and other harmful impacts such as pollution. Since their purpose is to stimulate sustainable behaviour rather than to increase state revenue, such taxes could replace existing taxes after a period of adjustment. Alternatively, the extra money raised could be returned as subsidies for more sustainable technology. The aim of taxes should be to raise them on behaviour that we want less of, such as the depletion of resources and pollution, and reduce them on what we want more of, such as employment. Resource taxes should be introduced gradually, over a period of ten years or more, to avoid economic disruption.

• Charges. Charges apply the User Pays Principle, and are useful for regulating access to shared resources. Examples are tourism fees for protected areas and water charges for irrigation. Pollution charges could also be levied, per unit of pollutant discharged. They should be more than it would cost to prevent the pollution in the first place. This should both motivate the industry concerned to prevent pollution and promote the development of anti-pollution technology.

• Subsidies. Subsidies can cover costs of achieving sustainability above the amount resource users can be expected to pay. They could, for example, help companies invest in the best pollution control equipment. Subsidies for unsustainable activities, such as grants or tax breaks to drain wetlands or clear forests, should be removed. They impose a double cost on society – the subsidy itself plus the cost of the damage it causes.

• Deposit/refund schemes. Under a deposit/refund scheme, a deposit is charged when an environmentally undesirable material or product is acquired, and refunded once the item has been disposed of properly. The scheme can work well with individuals as well as industry. It reduces the risk of people or companies avoiding high charges through illicit dumping of harmful waste (provided the deposit is more than the costs of disposing of the material in an approved way).

• Performance bonds. A performance bond is a kind of deposit/refund scheme in which companies that use or extract a resource have a deposit refunded when they have fulfilled certain management objectives. For example, bonds would be refunded when mining companies have completed site restoration work after the end of mining operations, or when forest has regenerated satisfactorily after timber cutting.

• Tradable permits. Tradable permits may be better than resource taxes in cases when it is important to establish a maximum overall level of emissions or resource use. A fixed quantity of permits to pollute or exploit a resource stock are allocated by auction, and enterprises are authorized to buy and sell them. Tradable permits are not appropriate for hazardous wastes, which should be dealt with stringently, and are usually regarded as a transition mechanism to avoid economic disruption until stricter standards can be attained.

Priority Actions

1
Adopt an integrated approach to environment policy

Governments, with public support, should set the creation of a sustainable society as an overall policy goal. To achieve it, they will need to ensure that all sectors of government consider the environmental impact of their activities. This is likely to require them to:
• Form a powerful inter-departmental sustainable development co-ordinating unit that is associated with the institutions responsible for finances and economic planning.
• Incorporate sustainability into the mandates and policies of departments and agencies
• Change the mandates of sectoral departments and agencies so that they become cross-sectoral
• Improve capacity to assess the environmental implications of proposed programmes and policies
• Adopt the precautionary principle in decision making
• Promote common approaches through policy forums that bring together representatives of government, environmental groups, business and industry, indigenous people and other interests on an equal footing.

2
Develop strategies for sustainability

Governments should develop national strategies for sustainability. By identifying the most urgent needs, they assist in setting priorities, allocating resources and building institutions capable of handling complex environmental issues. Important concerns should be that:
• Conservation and development problems are tackled in a comprehensive and integrated fashion
• Strategies for sustainability include a fundamental re-examination of policies, laws and institutions
• Strategies are prepared in collaboration with a wide array of interest groups
• Strategies are implemented through regional and local land-use plans designed in collaboration with local communities.

3
Subject proposals to Environmental Impact Assessment

An EIA is an important way of predicting and addressing the likely environmental consequences of proposed projects, programmes and policies, and should be an essential step in planning, It should:
• Be applied to proposals shown by preliminary screening as likely to have significant environmental, social or economic impacts
• Go beyond assessing and mitigating impacts of projects to assessing alternatives, including not proceeding with the project.
• Always be undertaken early in planning, at the feasibility stages
• Provide for the full public participation of all groups that might be affected
• Include an environmental management programme for all projects that go ahead
• Be subject to independent review.

4
Establish a constitutional commitment to sustainability

A commitment to the principles of a sustainable society should be incorporated in the constitution or other fundamental statements of national policy. It would oblige states to:
• Safeguard the human rights of citizens
• Protect future generations
• Conserve the nation's life-support systems and biodiversity
• Ensure that all uses of renewable resources are sustainable
• Provide for effective participation of communities and interest groups in the decisions that affect them.

5

Establish a comprehensive system of environmental law

Every nation should have rigorous environmental laws, covering:
• Land use and development planning
• Sustainable use of renewable and non-wasteful use of non-renewable resources
• Prevention of pollution, through the imposition of emission, environmental quality and product standards
• Efficient use of energy, through the establishment of efficiency standards
• Control of hazardous substances, including measures to prevent accidents
• Standards for minimizing waste and measures to promote recycling
• Conservation of species and ecosystems, through land-use management, specific measures to safeguard vulnerable species and the setting aside of protected areas
• Penalties to deter non-compliance
• Full and rapid compensation not only for economic losses suffered by other resource users, but for ecological and intangible losses
• Requirements that ecosystems should be restored so far as possible and that damages be paid if this is not possible.

6

Strengthen the knowledge base

Sustainability requires knowledge of the environmental matters and accessible information. Action is needed to:
• Strengthen research capacity, enabling research institutions to identify and define key tasks, carry out appropriate investigations, disseminate results and participate in international programmes
• Ensure new knowledge gets into the education and training system
• Make information about the environment freely available
• Ensure that information assembled by different agencies can be compared on a standardized basis and is combined in local and national databases
• Monitor indicators of environmental well-being and quality of life, as well as the performance of and public support for policies, laws and protection measures
• Collaborate internationally to develop standard research and monitoring methods and promote them world-wide
• Establish a programme of national auditing, with governments reporting regularly on the state of their environment and human development.

7

Use economic policies to achieve sustainability

All countries should use economic instruments as a means of promoting sustainability. They should:
• Adopt and implement the Polluter Pays Principle and the User Pays Principle
• Use charges, resource taxes, subsidies, tradeable permits and performance bonds as incentives for resource users
• Shelter certain sections of society from the full impact of extra costs through carefully targeted support schemes.

8

Ensure government economic decisions take full account of their effects on the environment

Governments should ensure that national policies, development plans, budgets and decisions on investments are in harmony with sustainability objectives by:
• Ensuring that environmental quality and natural resources are properly valued in national accounting
• Examining existing monetary and fiscal policies (such as subsidies and taxes) for their environmental impacts
• Evaluating the environmental costs of expenditure programmes before approval
• Using environmental and human development criteria to monitor progress.

Above left A freshly caught pirarucu is hauled ashore at a fish market in the varzea (flooded forest) region of northern Amazonia. Pirarucu were once plentiful, but overfishing has caused them to become endangered, and they are now found only in more remote areas. In many cases the survival of species that are hunted for food or other products can be ensured, at least in the short term, only through strictly enforced regulations.

Above High school students enjoy a game viewing drive as part of an environmental education workshop in Damaraland, Namibia. Sustainable living requires having a good knowledge of environmental matters.

Creating a Global Alliance

No nation today is self-sufficient. Global and shared resources, especially the atmosphere, oceans and shared ecosystems, can be managed only on the basis of common purpose and resolve. All nations stand to gain from the attainment of world-wide sustainability – and all are threatened if we fail to achieve it.

If we are to achieve global sustainability, a firm alliance must be established among all countries, with the backing of strong international law. Given the unequal levels of development in the world, the lower-income countries will need help to play their part to develop sustainably and protect their environments. The global alliance will also require the widest involvement, of not only national governments, but also citizens' groups, businesses and key international institutions.

Strengthening international law

A reshaping of international law is required to reflect the obligations nations have towards the Earth. Agreements to co-operate usually take the form of treaties, which may be bilateral (between two countries), multilateral or truly global. One of the first resource-management accords was the Boundary Waters Treaty of 1909, which provided a means of settling differences between Canada and the United States regarding the use of waters that flowed between the two countries.

During the ensuing decades, there was only a handful of treaties dealing with the environment and natural resources, but then interest began to mount. Whaling became the subject of agreement in 1946, pollution of the sea by oil in 1954 and the Antarctic in 1959. Beginning in the 1970s, some important agreements were negotiated. These included the Ramsar Convention on Wetlands (1971), the World Heritage Convention (1972), the Convention on the Dumping of Wastes at Sea (1972), the Convention on Trade in Endangered Species (CITES) (1973), the Convention for the Prevention of Pollution from Ships (1973), and the Convention on Migratory Species (1979).

The first convention relating to air quality, the Convention on Long Range Transboundary Air Pollution, was completed in Geneva in 1979. It is regional rather than global in application, but its benefits will be felt well beyond the countries to which it specifically applies. The issue that really made transboundary pollution a global issue was the depletion of the stratospheric ozone layer. This is a phenomenon for which practically all states are responsible, although to varying degrees, and which will have an effect in all states. The 1985 Vienna Convention for the protection of the ozone layer and subsequent protocols and amendments address this problem.

Antarctica and the Southern Ocean are home to 54 species of seabird and 21 marine mammals, including whales. Scientific activity and tourism have expanded rapidly, causing locally significant pollution. Some fish have been heavily exploited and the production of minerals has been seen as potentially a severe threat. Through international co-operation, Antarctica has always been demilitarized and nuclear free. In 1991, a protocol to the Antarctic Treaty was signed, enabling a regime for environmental conservation and a 50-year moratorium on mining and hydrocarbon production; it includes the first recognition of wilderness and aesthetic values in a major international convention.

Conventions are often difficult to conclude satisfactorily because they generally call for the politically sensitive sacrifice of short-term gain for the sake of long-term benefits. As a result, none of the conventions mentioned is ideal from the conservation point of view. Most are difficult to enforce.

None the less, all represent a start towards good management of the global environment and all provide a basis upon which improvements can be built. It is important that these existing measures are fully supported, maintained and implemented, and in some cases reinforced.

Left Icebergs and pack ice on the edge of Antarctica. The continent of Antarctica has a unique legal status, belonging to no country and having unusually stringent protection under international treaty. It is the only major landmass that has no permanent human population and is perhaps the greatest wilderness remaining on Earth. There has been considerable pressure for exploitation of the mineral resources thought to be on the continent, but this was banned for 50 years in 1991 by a protocol to the Antarctic Treaty. No doubt, however, such pressure will arise again as some resources run low in other regions of the world.

Below Nilgai in the Keoladeo National Park, Rajasthan, India. Under the Ramsar Convention on Wetlands, various regions, including Keoladeo, were designated as being of international importance. The convention was designed to provide international protection to wetland ecosystems.

Left Items seized under the 1973 Convention on Trade in Endangered Species (CITES) regulations at Hong Kong airport. Enforcement of CITES has caused considerable reduction in the traffic of a number of wildlife products. However, not all nations enforce the regulations with the same rigour, and many individuals will pay very high prices for what they consider to be desirable items.

If we are to achieve global sustainability, a firm alliance must be established among all countries

Further co-operation is needed on such issues as climate, biodiversity, forests and marine resources. Some agreement or negotiation has already taken place in a number of these areas – indeed, the first three were addressed during the run-up to the 1992 Earth Summit, where the biodiversity and climate change conventions were open for signature. However, concrete actions to implement them have not yet been taken.

Co-operation would be enhanced by a universal covenant on sustainability, which should take the form of a global declaration expressing a world ethic of living sustainably and the ensuing obligations. Such a covenant would be a framework for new accords and for states to consider environmental and development issues. It could also help in the creation of financial institutions for the support of global sustainability on the lines of the Global Environment Facility (see box).

The Global Environment Facility

The Global Environment Facility (GEF) has been set up on a pilot basis under an agreement made by 25 countries in 1990 and is managed by the World Bank, the United Nations Environment Programme and the United Nations Development Programme. The GEF provides funding for investments related to four objectives: limitation of greenhouse gas emissions by supporting energy conservation, alternative energy sources and forest management; preservation of areas that are rich in natural diversity; protection of international drainage basins and seas, particularly from transboundary pollution; and halting destruction of the ozone layer by helping countries use alternatives to CFCs and other ozone-depleting substances. Initial financial commitments to the GEF, however, have been far from sufficient for it to meet these objectives, nor has the GEF yet worked out satisfactory policies and mechanisms to govern its disbursements of funds. These problems are now being carefully evaluated.

Above Workers picking tea near Cibodas, Indonesia. Tea is almost entirely produced in lower-income countries as a crop for export. Although the foreign exchange earned may be welcome – often for debt repayments – reliance on such commodities can leave countries vulnerable to fluctuations in international trade conditions.

Far right Medical research in a laboratory to assess the potential of a new drug extracted from wild plants. Pharmaceutical companies have a strong motive to invest in the preservation of the environment and biodiversity. Plants have already provided the basis of many important drugs, and many more certainly await discovery.

Investing in environmental care

Clearly, the strength of the global alliance will be largely determined by how much money countries invest, both in their own and in co-operative efforts. Priority efforts would be to double the supply of family planning services, improve education, provide basic health care and sanitation, rehabilitate degraded environments, conserve biological diversity, sustain agricultural productivity, expand reafforestation, increase energy efficiency and develop renewable sources of energy.

The sums that are required globally are difficult to estimate, but will be large. One estimate calls for total expenditure of about $160 billion per annum by the year 2000.

High-income countries can be expected to meet all of their environmental investment needs; and most middle-income countries should be able to meet a substantial proportion of theirs. However, many lower-income and highly indebted countries cannot concentrate on sustainability because their resources must be directed towards more immediate preoccupations. They need economic reform and direct assistance.

Debt retirement and trade liberalization should go a long way towards reversing the present unacceptable resource flow from the lower-income to the higher-income countries. The most indebted regions are sub-Saharan Africa, where average debt now equals gross national product (GNP), and Latin America where it is 60 per cent of GNP. Massive debt repayments can force countries to curb living standards, accept growing poverty and export greater amounts of scarce resources, thus

accelerating environmental destruction. It is essential that the official debt (owed to governments and governmental banks) and commercial debt (owed to commercial banks) of lower-income countries be reduced. So-called debt-for-nature swaps, in which part of a debt is effectively written off in exchange for commitment by the debtor country to undertake environmental projects, can be a useful part of the debt retirement process. It is important, however, to avoid any semblance of imposed conditions that deny the debtor country full control over its own sustainability strategy.

Trade conditions for Third World countries must be improved. This involves reviewing farming subsidies in high-income countries, which create artificially low world prices and undermine the local and export markets of lower-income countries. Trade barriers that block Third World exports should be scrutinized. Only legitimate restrictions on trade, such as barriers to contaminated foodstuffs, should be kept. Fluctuations and speculation in currency, commodity prices and interest rates weaken vulnerable economies. Agreements are needed to support and stabilize the prices of the primary commodities on which so many developing countries rely.

At the same time, investment in lower-income countries should be encouraged. At present, profits from Latin American nations generally end up in United States and European banks (an example of what is known as "capital flight"). This is a denial of investment that may have as big an impact as debt. Investment must be of a kind that is neither exploitative nor environmentally damaging.

Ways of financing new investment

Below **Long-range missiles are paraded through Tehran, Iran. Like many countries, Iran has used a large part of its income for military spending. Diversion of large amounts of money from military budgets to deal with environmental problems that threaten regional security, would make better sense.**

• Transfers from military budgets. Land degradation, deforestation, global warming, competition for water, human population growth and movements of refugees pose major threats to national and regional security. Current world military expenditures do nothing to protect countries from these threats. Tackling them in peaceful ways would be a legitimate use of military budgets, which could cover the cost of a global sustainability strategy and still leave a huge remainder.

• Private sector investment services. These could foster private investment in conservation. The service would be similar to that of an investment bank, gathering capital, spreading risks, arranging access to technology, and improving incentives for investment in sustainable resource use.

• Earthcare bonds. These could be marketed to individuals and organizations wishing to make an affordable contribution to conservation and human development. Their sale would be used to build up a fund for investment, the proceeds of which would finance sustainable activities after providing modest returns to the bond-holders.

• Corporate contributions. Corporations in ten major industries – beverages, chemicals, clothing, food and confectionery, paper and wood products, pharmaceuticals, rubber and plastics, soaps and cosmetics, textiles and tobacco – depend wholly or partly on wild plants and animals for raw materials. They benefit from conservation of flora and fauna, but have not so far paid for it. It would be appropriate for them to help fund measures that maintain the wild gene pools, species and habitats that form resource bases of their industry. The Biodiversity Convention, not yet in place, will provide a mechanism for payment.

• Fund-raising schemes. These could raise substantial sums from individuals for essential actions. The schemes could include: a tax on tickets at major events, such as the Olympic Games and World Fairs; telethons and other fund-raising schemes; and an international lottery.

Assisting development

The use of development assistance programmes is the method that the high-income countries have designed to help the low-income countries with their development. Large sums are involved, major elements of infrastructure have been constructed and there have been significant transfers of goods and services. In 1990, official development assistance totalled over $62 billion. However, a long-standing target for the amount of development assistance to reach 0.7 per cent of GNP has been realized by only a very few of the high-income countries. Moreover, in recent years the flow of funds from lower-income to higher-income countries to repay debt has exceeded the flow of development assistance. The higher-income countries should recognize that it is in their own long-term interests to increase the funding and effectiveness of development assistance.

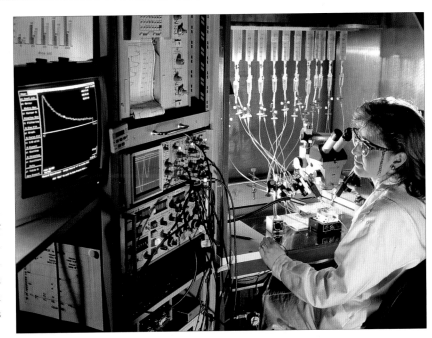

Many countries stipulate that their own products and the services of their own nationals must be used in implementing the assistance programmes that they have funded. This practice should not be allowed to prevent the development of skills and facilities within the recipient countries.

The style and impact of development assistance has also come under increasing criticism in recent years. Resettlement projects and dams have been particular targets for criticism. Several massive resettlement projects have failed to assess the carrying capacity of the areas to which the people have been moved. A number of major dams have been constructed without sufficient regard for either the environmental damage and the social distress that they have caused.

As a result, more attention is now being given to environmental and social factors in the planning and execution of major development projects. So-called mega-projects are no longer viewed as favourably as they once were. Another progressive move is that technical assistance – the delivery of know-how – is now accounting for a larger proportion of the total development assistance budget. This is the most valuable kind of aid available, because it increases a country's capacity to analyse and solve its own problems.

Right **Our hopes for the future. The Tree of Life outside the United Nations Conference on Environment and Development (UNCED), or the Earth Summit, held during June 1992 in Rio de Janeiro, Brazil. Children all over the world made leaves for the tree and sent them to Rio. Their involvement in such events, no matter how small, can only help increase their awareness of the importance of a global alliance.**

The Earth Summit

The United Nations Conference on Environment and Development (UNCED) – or the Earth Summit – was held in Rio de Janeiro, Brazil, in June 1992. It was attended by 114 heads of government and several thousand others. Participants included representatives of UN organizations, governments, NGOs and the media. The Global Forum, a parallel event, attracted thousands more concerned people from all over the world.

Although it was governments that authorized the Conference, the pressure to do so came from a steady increase in public concern. The hope was that the Earth Summit would not only define the steps needed to prevent further environmental deterioration, rehabilitate damaged ecosystems and enhance development, but also secure commitments to provide money for additional action and lay the basis for reforms in the UN system.

During the two-week Conference, delegates concluded five major agreements that had been arduously negotiated during the preceding several years. Two of the agreements are framework treaties. They set out the principles upon which action is to be based in a framework within which more detailed, action-oriented protocols have

then to be fitted. The Climate Change Convention, signed by 154 governments, is aimed primarily at slowing down and eventually halting global warming. The Biodiversity Convention, signed by 153 governments, is intended to preserve diversity among and within ecosystems and species. Both these conventions need to be ratified by at least 30 countries before they can come into effect.

The three other agreements reached at the Earth Summit were the Rio Declaration, Agenda 21 and the Statement of Forest Principles. Although these agreements are non-binding (governments are not legally obliged to implement what they propose), together with the statements

Above **Fidel Castro, President of Cuba, signs the Biodiversity Convention at the Earth Summit in Rio. The Summit was attended by more than a hundred heads of government and many nations sent senior representatives. The Biodiversity Convention was signed by 153 governments, although it still must be ratified by some of them before it can come into effect.**

A global alliance

An effective global alliance must harness the total resources of humanity to deal with the immense challenges of the coming decades. This means national governments collaborating fully with intergovernmental bodies, NGOs, the indigenous and religious groups, and the world of business, industry and commerce. All have to work together to solve problems and promote changing patterns. There should also be a joint approach to monitoring and research, shared between official and non-governmental bodies, to create an increasingly reliable common body of knowledge.

At the intergovernmental level, the United Nations (UN) has been instrumental in addressing some key issues, but it is hampered by its division into sectors. Each organization within the UN has its own particular field of concern and its own autonomous legislative body, resulting in policies that sometimes have conflicting aims. Action is needed to strengthen and streamline the UN machinery to ensure a co-ordinated approach based on an agenda determined by the widest practicable discussion. Such concerns were reflected in the 1992 United Nations Conference on Environment and Development (UNCED), often referred to as the Earth Summit (see box below).

Above Visitors to the United Nations building in New York. The UN is the world's leading intergovernmental body and has achieved much in bringing together differing interests and providing a unified international voice. There are, however, structural problems within the UN, largely the result of failure to co-ordinate the work of its many agencies.

made to the Conference by government leaders, they constitute a moral commitment that governments will find difficult to ignore. Thousands of NGOs throughout the world will be closely watching the performance of their governments during the next few years.

The Rio Declaration is a statement of 27 principles upon which societies should base attempts to achieve development that is sustainable. Agenda 21 is an 800-page, detailed programme for dealing with environmental and developmental problems. It is an invaluable reference for the actions that will be needed in the next decade and is intended as a guide for international organizations

and for national governments. The Statement of Forest Principles is just what its name implies; because it was agreed as non-binding, it is, in a sense, a convention still in the making.

While the Earth Summit accomplished a good deal, much still remains to be done. As UNCED Secretary General, Maurice Strong, said, "Rio helped to set direction and energize the political process, but its promise will not be realized unless people make it happen where they are – in corporations, in communities, in their own lives."

Throughout its course, the Earth Summit debate was preoccupied with immediate practical and political issues: little attention was given to more fundamental concerns such as the links between population, resources, environment and development, and the need to work towards social, economic and ecological sustainability.

Before they can be put into effect, all the agreements reached at Rio need to be followed up with a detailed consideration of priorities and funding sources by each participating body. Put another way, countries and international organizations will need to develop strategies for sustainable living along the lines set out in this book.

Priority Actions

1

Strengthen existing international agreements

Many international agreements deal with the environment, on issues including air and water pollution, hazardous wastes, and species protection. States should:
• Maintain or give their support for international agreements
• Enact domestic legislation and commit resources to carry out their obligations
• Assist lower-income countries with the work of implementation.

2

Conclude new international agreements to help achieve global sustainability

The preparation and implementation of new agreements are vital. Governments should give priority to the following:
• Ratification and implementation of the 1992 Biodiversity Convention
• Ratification and implementation of the 1992 Climate Change Convention
• Commitments to collaborate on safeguarding the world's forests
• Bringing into force the UN Convention on the Law of the Sea.

3

Prepare and adopt a Universal Declaration and Covenant on Sustainability

This Covenant should be the expression in international law of the world ethics for living sustainably. It would reflect the commitment of states to the principles of those ethics and define their corresponding rights and duties. The Covenant should:
• Express the need to safeguard the environmental rights of future generations, maintain the productivity and diversity of the Earth and treat other species ethically
• Express the commitments and corresponding obligations of states to live sustainably, and to care for their national environmental resources
• Emphasize the responsibilities of all states to protect the global commons and shared resources
• Propose procedures for settling international disputes over environmental and resource issues.

4

Reduce the debt of lower-income countries

To restore economic progress to lower-income countries, it is important that higher-income countries:
• All write off the official debt of low-income countries
• Set up a fund to retire much of their commercial debt
• Ensure this debt relief is additional to other forms of development assistance
• Negotiate for funds released by retiring debt to be used to support strategies for sustainability by the debtor nation.

5

Increase the capacity of lower-income countries to help themselves

Economic growth and sustainable environmental management in lower-income countries would be facilitated by:
• Removing trade barriers to their exports to help them obtain greater benefits from their natural resources (unless these are legitimate restrictions for environmental or health reasons)
• Supporting and stabilizing the prices of the commodities they export through, for example, international agreements
• Removing farm subsidies that encourage overproduction in upper-income countries (and redirecting them to farmers who practise conservation)
• Encouraging investment in their economies and limiting capital flight from lower- to upper-income countries.

Above Collecting roots for food in the drought-stricken south of Madagascar. Crises such as drought often stimulate considerable international relief efforts. However, the solution to relieving such problems must ultimately lie in much more long-term measures that would allow countries to make their own preparations for times of crisis, and to try to avoid crises altogether. This kind of measure should include reforms in international trade and development aid.

Top right A waterfall on the slopes of Mount Kenya. In a scene of great natural beauty, water and rock form a rich variety of habitats for plant and animal life. A global alliance is necessary if such scenes are to be there for our descendants to see.

6

Increase and redirect development assistance

Aid agencies should increase the flow of development assistance and devote it to helping countries develop sustainable societies and economies. High priority should be given to:
• Building countries' institutional and technical capacity (organization, knowledge and skills) for undertaking sustainable development
• Increasing the assistance given to social reform programmes
• Ensuring the participation of the communities that will be affected in the design and implementation of projects and programmes
• Changing the mode of lending from project to programme (e.g. providing funds for a general forest programme), leaving the recipient government to devise individual projects; the funds could be paid in instalments as agreed programme targets are met
• Increasing the number of small-scale projects and ensuring that they have maximum grassroots participation
• Assessing, disclosing and taking full account of the environmental impacts of programmes as well as projects.

7

Strengthen global and national non-governmental action

Global sustainability will be achieved only if it is pursued by people throughout all nations. Citizens' groups, especially those concerned with conservation and development, have a vital part to play because they are familiar with the issues, have the expertise to bring to bear, and have both commitment and flexibility. NGOs can take the lead in:
• Convening forums at national and regional levels, involving the governmental and non-governmental sectors, business and industry
• Organizing workshops and groups of experts to evaluate key issues, provide reports and brief the media
• Preparing strategies for sustainability
• Undertaking demonstration projects and providing suggestions for actions to governments or local communities that they will then be able to take up and develop for themselves.

8

Make the United Nations system an effective force for global sustainability

The UN system has promoted and assisted better management of the environment and natural resources. However, the division of organizations by sector, within both national governments and the UN itself, has impeded progress. Governments should:
• Redefine the mandates of the UN agencies and impose a collective responsibility on them to work for sustainability in a co-ordinated way
• Ensure that their own representatives to the UN agencies pursue consistent policies. The UN system should:
• Adopt an integrated approach to the environment and to sustainability, using inter-agency policies laid down at the highest level
• Provide annual reports on the global environment, signed jointly by the heads of the UN and other participating bodies, covering issues requiring urgent international co-operation and setting out the main policy options for action.

Index

Acknowledgements

The publisher would like to thank the following organizations and individuals for providing the photographs used in this book:

Andes Press Agency /Carlos Reyes 1; Bruce Colman Ltd. 112; Ecoscene /Winkley 85t; Environmental Picture Library /Martin Bond 139, /Graham Burns 16bl, /Philip Carr 124t, /P. Fryer 71l, /Stan Gamester 122-23b; Roger Few 30-31, 44, 56-57; Hutchison Library /Edward Parker 15, /Singer 14bl; Impact /Peter Arkell 45b, 47t, /Bureau Bangkok 46t, /Gerald Buthaud 2-3, /Piers Cavendish 36, 40t, /Christopher Cormack 46-47, /Ben Edwards 32-33, /Sally Fear 142t, /Rhonda Klevansky 23r, /Moradabadi 28-29, 151t, /Richard McCraig 58, /Caroline Penn 42, /Roger Scruton 141r, /Homer Sykes 140; ISE Photo Library 29r; IUCN 104t; Magnum /Chris Steele-Perkins 8-9, 43; NAWCC 104t; NHPA /Stephen Krasemann 98c; Panos Pictures /Neil Cooper 49b, 134t, /Martin Flitman 10b, Jeremy Hartley 134-35, /Alain Le Garsmeur 34, /David Reed 63, /Sean Sprague 138l, /Katharine Wratten 46c; Reed International Books Ltd. /Cliff Webb 113b; Rex Features /Edward Igor 142-43, /Sipa Press 153; Science Photo Library /Mark Burnett 144t, /Will McIntyre 120-21, /NASA 145, /Geoff Tompkinson 151b; Select /UNEP /Kurt Adams 113tl; Still Pictures /Mark Edwards 19t, 35t; Tessa Traeger 52-53; WWF 13bl, 321, 67b, 85b, 88-89, /Christer Agren 66-67, /Daniel Aubort 149r, /André Bärtschi 52, 102l, /Luc Bertau 78tl, /Mark Boulton 12-13, 18, 25b, 74-75, 133r, /Alain Compost 11r, 87r, /Gerald Cubitt 144b, /Michele Depraz 24-25, 140-41, /M. Donoghue 114t, /Long Earshal 69t,

/Mark Edwards 10-11t, 16br, 38l, 45t, 70l, 81b, 90b, 97b, 99t, 132r, /D. L. Elder 130b, /Paul Forster 49t, 69b, 105t, 121, 124b, /M. Franck 116, /Werner Gartung 17, 22b, 68, 105b, 125l, 138r, /Meg Gawler 501, /Michel Gunther 21r, 54-55, 72-73 /D. Halleux 26tl, 26tr, 113b, /Peter Jackson 75t, 148b, /Hartmut Jungius 89b, 92, 94l, 106-7, 122-23t, 136b, /Jacqueline Kaufmann 102r, 111b, /Mikaail Kavanagh 100t, /Elizabeth Kemf 14r, /Klein & Hubert 331, /Matthias Klum 6-7, /B. & C. Lang 111c, /Oliver Langrand 131, /Roger Le Guen 55, 117, /Marek Libersky 19b, 120l, /Sandra Mbanefo 39, 59, 64b, 66b, 1321, 147, /D. Miller & S. Frank 109, /Alan Moore 22-23, /Tom Moss 118b, 150, /John Newby 26-27, 40b, 51, 60, 861, 86-87, 96-97, 100b, 103, 114b, 126-27, 128t, 128b, 1331, 154, /Frank Nowikowski 80-81, 83c, /Philippe Oberle 64-65, 155, /Brent Occleshaw 21b, /Edward Parker 50r, 94-95, 98-99, 106t, 146, /Ron Petocz 110-11, /Jonathan Plant 73b, 94b, /Juan G. Pratginestos 28b, 62, 76, 93, 152t, 152b, /Tony Rath 20-21, 110l, /Mauri Rautkari 13br, 27r, 38r, 53b, 61, 84r, 88t, 78b, 70-71, 74t, 96b, 101, 104-5, 107b, 122l, 136t, 137, /Don Reid 58-59, /Willem F. Rodenburg 72t, /William Rossiter 113r, /Albrecht G. Schaefer 91t, /Soh Koon Chng 37, 77, 84l, /Jack Stein Grove 82-83, 125r, 148-49, /Jim Thorsell 129, 130t, /Albert Visage 10tl, 118-19, /Rob Webster 20t, 56, 78-79, /Rick Weyerhaeuser 115, /J. L. Ziegler 41, /A. E. Zuckerman 48, 83b.

Illustrations: Colin Rose; Ed Stuart   **Thanks to** Caroline Wollen